TO

_____

FROM

_____

DATE

_____

30 Lessons from The Life of Christ

Dr. Criswell Freeman

30 Lessons from The Life of Christ

Dr. Criswell Freeman

TABLE OF CONTENTS

INTRODUCTION

I f you're like most people, you simply can't remember the first time you heard the name Jesus—His name, like His Good News, is likely woven into the fabric of your life. But perhaps you haven't thought as much about the lessons that you can learn from the life and the words of Jesus. If so, this book can help.

This text examines 30 lessons from the life and the teachings of Jesus. That means that for the next month you'll have 30 different opportunities to consider the role that Christ plays in your life today, and the role that you intend for Him to play tomorrow.

Hannah Whitall Smith correctly observed, "The crucial question for each of us is this: What do you think of Jesus, and do you yet have a personal acquaintance with Him?" How do you answer that question? Do you have a personal acquaintance with the carpenter from Galilee, and are you a different person because of that relationship? During the next 30 days, you'll be asked to think carefully about your answer.

As you read this text, take time to consider the role that Jesus plays in your life—and, more importantly, the role that He should play. Be mindful of Christ's lessons, and apply them. When you do, you'll be blessed today, tomorrow, and forever.

A TIMELINE
OF THE LIFE OF JESUS

(Dates Are Approximate)

6/5 BC: Jesus is born in Bethlehem.

6/5 BC: Jesus is presented in the temple at Jerusalem.

6/5 BC: Mary and Joseph escape with the baby Jesus to Egypt.

6/5 BC: Mary and Joseph return to Nazareth with the baby Jesus.

7/8 AD: A young Jesus goes to the temple in Jerusalem.

26: AD: Jesus is baptized by John in the Jordan River.

26 AD: In the wilderness, Jesus is tempted by Satan.

26 AD: Jesus performs His first miracle at Cana by turning water into wine.

27 AD: Jesus removes money changers from the temple.

27 AD: Jesus heals the sick and performs other miracles.

27-28 AD: Jesus gains followers and chooses 12 disciples.

28 AD: Jesus preaches the Sermon on the Mount at Capernaum

28 AD: Jesus travels through Galilee teaching and performing miracles.

28 AD: Jesus sends His disciples to preach and heal.

28 AD: John the Baptist is killed by Herod.

29 AD: Jesus feeds the 5,000, walks on water, and performs other miracles.

29 AD: Jesus tells His disciples He will die soon.

29 AD: Jesus visits Mary and Martha; He raises Lazarus from the dead.

30 AD: Jesus makes His triumphal return to Jerusalem.

30 AD: The Last Supper

30 AD: Jesus is crucified and buried on a Friday. On Sunday He rises from the dead and appears to His followers. 40 days later He ascends to heaven.

Source: Biblenet.net

CHRIST OFFERS ETERNAL LIFE

Jesus said to her, "I am the resurrection and the life.
The one who believes in Me, even if he dies, will live.
Everyone who lives and believes in Me will never die—ever.
Do you believe this?"

John 11:25-26 Holman CSB

The Message

Jesus makes an amazing promise: those who believe in
Him will receive the priceless gift of eternal life.

How marvelous it is that God became a man and walked among us. Had He not chosen to do so, we might feel removed from a distant Creator. But ours is not a distant God. Ours is a God who understands—far better than we ever could—the essence of what it means to be human.

God understands our hopes, our fears, and our temptations. He understands what it means to be angry and what it costs to forgive. He knows the heart, the conscience, and the soul of every person who has ever lived, including you. And God has a plan of salvation that is intended for you. Accept it. Accept God's gift through the person of His Son Christ Jesus, and then rest assured: God walked among us so that you might have eternal life; amazing though it may seem, He did it for you.

> *And we have seen and testify that the Father has sent his Son to be the Savior of the world.*
> 1 John 4:14 NIV

As mere mortals, our vision for the future, like our lives here on earth, is limited. God's vision is not burdened by such limitations: His plans extend throughout all eternity. Thus, God's plans for you are not limited to the ups and downs of everyday life. Your Heavenly Father has bigger things in mind . . . much bigger things.

Let us praise the Creator for His priceless gift, and let us share the Good News with all who cross our paths.

We return our Father's love by accepting His grace and by sharing His message and His love. When we do, we are blessed here on earth and throughout all eternity.

As you struggle with the inevitable hardships and occasional disappointments of life, remember that God has invited you to accept His abundance not only for today but also for all eternity. So keep things in perspective. Although you will inevitably encounter occasional defeats in this world, you'll have all eternity to celebrate the ultimate victory in the next.

A LESSON TO THINK ABOUT

If you have already welcomed Christ into your heart as your personal Savior, then you are safe. If you're still sitting on the fence, the time to accept Him is this very moment.

WHAT GOD'S WORD SAYS ABOUT SALVATION

Blessed be the God and Father of our Lord Jesus Christ, who according to His great mercy has caused us to be born again to a living hope through the resurrection of Jesus Christ from the dead.

1 Peter 1:3 NASB

Here is a trustworthy saying that deserves full acceptance: Christ Jesus came into the world to save sinners—of whom I am the worst.

1 Timothy 1:15 NIV

The sun will be turned into darkness, and the moon will turn bloodred, before that great and glorious day of the Lord arrives. And anyone who calls on the name of the Lord will be saved.

Acts 2:20-21 NLT

It is by the name of Jesus Christ of Nazareth . . . Salvation is found in no one else, for there is no other name under heaven given to men by which we must be saved.

Acts 4:10,12 NIV

WORDS OF WISDOM ABOUT SALVATION

Personal salvation is not an occasional rendezvous with Deity; it is an actual dwelling with God.

Billy Graham

God's goal is not to make you happy. It is to make you his.

Max Lucado

Our salvation comes to us so easily because it cost God so much.

Oswald Chambers

Today is the day of salvation. Some people miss heaven by only eighteen inches—the distance between their heads and their hearts.

Corrie ten Boom

I have been all over the world, and I have never met anyone who regretted giving his or her life to Christ.

Billy Graham

Notes to Yourself: _____

_____

_____

_____

_____

_____

_____

_____

_____

_____

_____

_____

_____

_____

As you consider the things you've written in the space above, ask yourself these questions:

Do I believe that God offers me the gift of eternal life through the sacrifice of His Son Jesus?

Am I confident about my relationship with Jesus, and do I believe that I will spend eternity with Him in heaven?

Does God's promise of salvation give me comfort and peace?

GOD'S LOVE IS YOUR SECURITY

"My son," the father said, "you are always with me, and everything I have is yours."

Luke 15:31 NIV

The Message

God's children are secure because He loves them, because He is near to them, and because He has all the resources they need for happiness and fulfillment.

God loves us, and He gives us strength. When every earthly support system fails, God remains steadfast, and His love remains unchanged. When we encounter life's inevitable disappointments and setbacks, God remains faithful. When we suffer losses that leave us breathless, God is always with us, always ready to respond to our prayers, always working in us and through us to turn tragedy into triumph.

God's love for you is bigger and better than you can imagine. In fact, God's love is far too big to comprehend (in this lifetime). But this much we know: God loves you so much that He sent His Son Jesus to come to this earth and to die for you. And, if you've allowed Jesus to reign over your life and your heart, you have already received a gift that is more precious than gold: the gift of eternal life.

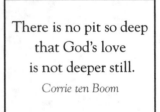

There is no pit so deep that God's love is not deeper still.

Corrie ten Boom

The words of Romans 8 make this promise: "For I am persuaded that neither death nor life, nor angels nor principalities nor powers, nor things present, nor things to come, nor height nor depth, nor any other created thing, shall be able to separate us from the love of God which is in Christ Jesus our Lord" (vv. 38-39 NKJV).

Sometimes, in the crush of your daily duties, God may seem far away, but He is not. God is everywhere you have ever been and everywhere you will ever go. He is with you night and day; He knows your thoughts and He hears your prayers. When you earnestly seek Him, you will find Him because He is here, waiting patiently for you to reach out to Him.

Reach out to God today and always. Encourage your family members to do likewise. And then, arm-in-arm with your loved ones, praise God for blessings that are simply too numerous to count.

A LESSON TO THINK ABOUT

When all else fails, God's love does not. You can always depend upon God's love . . . and He is always your ultimate protection.

WHAT GOD'S WORD SAYS ABOUT GOD'S LOVE

We know how much God loves us, and we have put our trust in him. God is love, and all who live in love live in God, and God lives in them.

1 John 4:16 NLT

As the Father loved Me, I also have loved you; abide in My love.

John 15:9 NKJV

For God so loved the world, that he gave his only begotten Son, that whosoever believeth in him should not perish, but have everlasting life.

John 3:16 KJV

The unfailing love of the LORD never ends! By his mercies we have been kept from complete destruction.

Lamentations 3:22 NLT

His banner over me was love.

Song of Solomon 2:4 KJV

WORDS OF WISDOM ABOUT GOD'S LOVE

The fact is, God no longer deals with us in judgment but in mercy. If people got what they deserved, this old planet would have ripped apart at the seams centuries ago. Praise God that because of His great love "we are not consumed, for His compassions never fail" (Lam. 3:22).

Joni Eareckson Tada

Being loved by Him whose opinion matters most gives us the security to risk loving, too—even loving ourselves.

Gloria Gaither

Even when we cannot see the why and wherefore of God's dealings, we know that there is love in and behind them, so we can rejoice always.

J. I. Packer

God proved His love on the cross. When Christ hung, and bled, and died, it was God saying to the world—I love you.

Billy Graham

Notes to Yourself: _____

_____

_____

_____

_____

_____

_____

_____

_____

_____

_____

_____

_____

_____

As you consider the things you've written in the space above, ask yourself these questions:

Do I believe that God loves me . . . and am I willing to return His love?

Am I willing to place God first in my life?

Am I genuinely fearful of disobeying God's commandments?

FAITH MOVES MOUNTAINS

I assure you: If anyone says to this mountain,
"Be lifted up and thrown into the sea," and does not
doubt in his heart, but believes that what
he says will happen, it will be done for him.

Mark 11:23 Holman CSB

The Message

Jesus promises that if you possess genuine, life-changing faith, you can move mountains for God.

The words of Jesus are clear: if you have faith, you can do miraculous things. And that's good because you live in a world where lots of mountains need to be moved.

Are you a mountain mover whose faith is evident for all to see? Or, are you a spiritual shrinking violet? God needs more men and women who are willing to move mountains for His glory and for His kingdom.

Jesus taught His disciples that if they had faith, they could move mountains. You can too. When you place your faith, your trust, indeed your life in the hands of Christ Jesus, you'll be amazed at the marvelous things He can do.

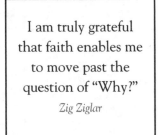

I am truly grateful that faith enables me to move past the question of "Why?"

Zig Ziglar

So strengthen your faith through praise, through worship, through Bible study, and through prayer. And trust God's plans. With Him, all things are possible, and He stands ready to open a world of possibilities to you . . . if you have faith.

Concentration camp survivor Corrie ten Boom relied on faith during her long months of imprisonment and torture. Later, despite the fact that four of her family members had died in Nazi death camps, Corrie's faith was unshaken. She wrote, "There is no pit so deep that God's love is not deeper still." Christians take note: Genuine faith in God means faith in all circumstances, happy or sad, joyful or tragic.

If your faith is being tested to the point of breaking, remember that your Savior is near. If you reach out to Him in faith, He will give you peace and strength. Reach out today. If you touch even the smallest fragment of the Master's garment, He will make you whole. And then, with no further ado, let the mountain moving begin.

A LESSON TO THINK ABOUT

If you don't have faith, you'll never move mountains. But if you do have faith, there's no limit to the things that you and God, working together, can accomplish.

WHAT GOD'S WORD SAYS ABOUT FAITH

For whatever is born of God overcomes the world. And this is the victory that has overcome the world—our faith.

1 John 5:4 NKJV

It is impossible to please God apart from faith. And why? Because anyone who wants to approach God must believe both that he exists and that he cares enough to respond to those who seek him.

Hebrews 11:6 MSG

Anything is possible if a person believes.

Mark 9:23 NLT

Fight the good fight of faith; take hold of the eternal life to which you were called . . . .

1 Timothy 6:12 NASB

Have faith in the LORD your God and you will be upheld . . . .

2 Chronicles 20:20 NIV

Words of Wisdom About Faith

There are a lot of things in life that are difficult to understand. Faith allows the soul to go beyond what the eyes can see.

John Maxwell

The popular idea of faith is of a certain obstinate optimism: the hope, tenaciously held in the face of trouble, that the universe is fundamentally friendly and things may get better.

J. I. Packer

When you enroll in the "school of faith," you never know what may happen next. The life of faith presents challenges that keep you going—and keep you growing!

Warren Wiersbe

Nothing is more disastrous than to study faith, analyze faith, make noble resolves of faith, but never actually to make the leap of faith.

Vance Havner

Notes to Yourself: _____

_____

_____

_____

_____

_____

_____

_____

_____

_____

_____

As you consider the things you've written in the space above, ask yourself these questions:

Am I willing to ask God to become a full partner in my work?

Am I willing to pray as if everything depended upon God and work as if everything depended upon me?

After I've done my best, am I willing to trust God's plan and His timetable for my life?

USE THE TALENTS GOD HAS GIVEN YOU

His master replied, "Well done, good and faithful servant!
You have been faithful with a few things;
I will put you in charge of many things.
Come and share your master's happiness!"

Matthew 25:21 NIV

The Message

In the Parable of the Talents, Jesus instructs us to take the right kinds of risks so that we might enhance our skills and serve our Creator.

God knew precisely what He was doing when He gave you a unique set of talents and opportunities. And now, God wants you to use those talents for the glory of His kingdom. So here's the big question: will you choose to use those talents, or not?

Your Heavenly Father wants you to be a faithful steward of the gifts He has given you. But you live in a society that may encourage you to do otherwise. You face countless temptations to squander your time, your resources, and your talents. So you must be keenly aware of the inevitable distractions that can waste your time, your energy, and your opportunities.

If you want to reach your potential, you need to add a strong work ethic to your talent.

John Maxwell

In the 25th chapter of Matthew, Jesus tells the "Parable of the Talents." In it, He describes a master who leaves his servants with varying amounts of money (talents). When the master returns, some servants have put their money to work and earned more, to which the master responds, "Well done . . . come and share your master's happiness!" (v. 25 NIV)

But the story does not end so happily for the foolish servant who was given a single talent but did nothing with it. For this man, the master has nothing but reproach: "You wicked, lazy servant . . ." (v. 26 NIV). The message from Jesus is clear: We must use our talents, not waste them.

Every day of your life, you have a choice to make: to nurture your talents or neglect them. When you choose wisely, God rewards your efforts, and He expands your opportunities to serve Him.

God has blessed you with unique opportunities to serve Him, and He has given you every tool that you need to do so. Today, accept this challenge: value the talent that God has given you, nourish it, make it grow, and share it with the world. After all, the best way to say "Thank You" for God's gifts is to use them.

A LESSON TO THINK ABOUT

If you are a disciple of the risen Christ, you have every reason on earth—and in heaven—to live courageously. And that's precisely what you should do.

WHAT GOD'S WORD SAYS ABOUT TALENTS

According to the grace given to us, we have different gifts: If prophecy, use it according to the standard of faith; if service, in service; if teaching, in teaching; if exhorting, in exhortation; giving, with generosity; leading, with diligence; showing mercy, with cheerfulness.

Romans 12:6-8 Holman CSB

I remind you to fan into flame the gift of God.

2 Timothy 1:6 NIV

Each man has his own gift from God; one has this gift, another has that.

1 Corinthians 7:7 NIV

Do not neglect the gift that is in you.

1 Timothy 4:14 Holman CSB

Thanks be to God for his indescribable gift!

2 Corinthians 9:15 NIV

WORDS OF WISDOM ABOUT TALENTS

Employ whatever God has entrusted you with, in doing good, all possible good, in every possible kind and degree.

John Wesley

God often reveals His direction for our lives through the way He made us . . . with a certain personality and unique skills.

Bill Hybels

Almighty God created us, redeemed us, called us, endowed us with gifts and abilities and perceptions. To demean the gift is to insult the Giver.

Penelope Stokes

One thing taught large in the Holy Scriptures is that while God gives His gifts freely, He will require a strict accounting of them at the end of the road. Each man is personally responsible for his store, be it large or small, and will be required to explain his use of it before the judgment seat of Christ.

A. W. Tozer

Notes to Yourself: _____

_____

_____

_____

_____

_____

_____

_____

_____

_____

_____

_____

_____

As you consider the things you've written in the space above, ask yourself these questions:

Am I making the most of my talents?

Am I willing to take sensible risks in the pursuit of spiritual and personal growth?

Is the fear of failure holding me back?

DON'T WORRY

But seek first the kingdom of God and His righteousness,
and all these things shall be added to you.
Therefore do not worry about tomorrow,
for tomorrow will worry about its own things.
Sufficient for the day is its own trouble.

Matthew 6:33-34 NKJV

The Message

As citizens of our modern, market-driven world, we're tempted to worry about food, fashion, fads, and almost everything else, for that matter. But if we're wise, we learn to worry less by seeking God's kingdom first. When we do, everything else falls into place.

Have you acquired the habit of worrying about almost everything under the sun? If so, it's a habit you should break.

Even if you're a very faithful Christian, you may be plagued by occasional periods of discouragement and doubt. Even though you trust God's promise of salvation—even though you sincerely believe in God's love and protection— you may find yourself upset by the countless details of everyday life. Jesus understood your concerns when He spoke the reassuring words found in the 6th chapter of Matthew:

> *Refrain from anger and turn from wrath; do not fret—it leads only to evil.*
> Psalm 37:8 NIV

"Therefore I say to you, do not worry about your life, what you will eat or what you will drink; nor about your body, what you will put on. Is not life more than food and the body more than clothing? Look at the birds of the air, for they neither sow nor reap nor gather into barns; yet your heavenly Father feeds them. Are you not of more value than they?" (vv. 25-27 NKJV)

Where is the best place to take your worries? Take them to God. Take your troubles to Him; take your fears to Him; take your doubts to Him; take your weaknesses to Him; take your sorrows to Him . . . and leave them all there. Seek protection from the One who offers you eternal salvation;

build your spiritual house upon the Rock that cannot be moved.

Perhaps you are concerned about your future, your relationships, or your finances. Or perhaps you are simply a "worrier" by nature. If so, choose to make Matthew 6 a regular part of your daily Bible reading. This beautiful passage will remind you that God still sits in His heaven and you are His beloved child. Then, perhaps, you will worry a little less and trust God a little more, and that's as it should be because God is trustworthy . . . and you are protected.

A LESSON TO THINK ABOUT

You have worries, but God has solutions. Your challenge it to trust Him to solve the problems that you can't.

WHAT GOD'S WORD SAYS ABOUT WORRY

Cast your burden upon the Lord and He will sustain you: He will never allow the righteous to be shaken.

Psalm 55:22 NASB

Don't worry about anything, but in everything, through prayer and petition with thanksgiving, let your requests be made known to God.

Philippians 4:6 Holman CSB

Yea, though I walk through the valley of the shadow of death, I will fear no evil: for thou art with me; thy rod and thy staff they comfort me.

Psalm 23:4 KJV

I will be with you when you pass through the waters . . . when you walk through the fire . . . the flame will not burn you. For I the Lord your God, the Holy One of Israel, and your Savior.

Isaiah 43:2-3 Holman CSB

WORDS OF WISDOM ABOUT WORRY

Worry is the senseless process of cluttering up tomorrow's opportunities with leftover problems from today.

Barbara Johnson

Never yield to gloomy anticipation. Place your hope and confidence in God. He has no record of failure.

Mrs. Charles E. Cowman

Pray, and let God worry.

Martin Luther

Today is mine. Tomorrow is none of my business. If I peer anxiously into the fog of the future, I will strain my spiritual eyes so that I will not see clearly what is required of me now.

Elisabeth Elliott

Worry and anxiety are sand in the machinery of life; faith is the oil.

E. Stanley Jones

Notes to Yourself: _____

_____

_____

_____

_____

_____

_____

_____

_____

_____

_____

_____

_____

As you consider the things you've written in the space above, ask yourself these questions:

Am I willing to trust God in every season of life, in good times and hard times?

Do I use faith as an antidote to worry?

Am I willing to trust God's Word, and do I expect Him to fulfill His promises?

IF YOU WISH TO FOLLOW JESUS, YOU MUST BE A SERVANT

Next, He poured water into a basin and began to wash His disciples' feet and to dry them with the towel tied around Him.

John 13:5 Holman CSB

The Message

Jesus, in one of His last acts here on earth, washed the feet of His disciples. By doing so, He taught them that they, too, must be servants. And, of course, Christ's message still applies.

We live in a world that glorifies power, prestige, fame, and money. But the words of Jesus teach us that the most esteemed men and women are not the widely acclaimed leaders of society; the most esteemed among us are the humble servants of society.

When we experience success, it's easy to puff out our chests and proclaim, "I did that!" But it's wrong. Whatever "it" is, God did it, and He deserves the credit. As Christians, we have been refashioned and saved by Jesus Christ, and that salvation came not because of our own good works but because of God's grace.

> If you aren't serving, you're just existing, because life is meant for ministry.
>
> *Rick Warren*

Dietrich Bonhoeffer was correct when he observed, "It is very easy to overestimate the importance of our own achievements in comparison with what we owe others." In other words, reality breeds humility.

Are you willing to become a humble servant for Christ? Are you willing to pitch in and make the world a better place, or are you determined to keep all your blessings to yourself? The answer to these questions will determine the quantity and the quality of the service you render to God—and to His children.

Today, you may feel the temptation to take more than you give. You may be tempted to withhold your generosity. Or you may be tempted to build yourself up in the eyes of your friends. Resist these temptations. Instead, serve your friends quietly and without fanfare. Find a need and fill it . . . humbly. Lend a helping hand . . . anonymously. Share a word of kindness . . . with quiet sincerity. As you go about your daily activities, remember that the Savior of all humanity made Himself a servant, and you, as His follower, must do no less.

A LESSON TO THINK ABOUT

Whether you realize it or not, God has called you to a life of service. Your job is to find a place to serve and to get busy.

WHAT GOD'S WORD SAYS ABOUT SERVICE

Worship the Lord your God and . . . serve Him only.

Matthew 4:10 Holman CSB

A person should consider us in this way: as servants of Christ and managers of God's mysteries. In this regard, it is expected of managers that each one be found faithful.

1 Corinthians 4:1-2 Holman CSB

If they serve Him obediently, they will end their days in prosperity and their years in happiness.

Job 36:11 Holman CSB

We must do the works of Him who sent Me while it is day. Night is coming when no one can work.

John 9:4 Holman CSB

Serve the Lord with gladness.

Psalm 100:2 Holman CSB

WORDS OF WISDOM ABOUT
SERVICE

Through our service to others, God wants to influence our world for Him.

Vonette Bright

God will open up places of service for you as He sees you are ready. Meanwhile, study the Bible and give yourself a chance to grow.

Warren Wiersbe

Christianity, in its purest form, is nothing more than seeing Jesus. Christian service, in its purest form, is nothing more than imitating him who we see. To see his Majesty and to imitate him: that is the sum of Christianity.

Max Lucado

So many times we say that we can't serve God because we aren't whatever is needed. We're not talented enough or smart enough or whatever. But if you are in covenant with Jesus Christ, He is responsible for covering your weaknesses, for being your strength. He will give you His abilities for your disabilities!

Kay Arthur

Notes to Yourself: _____

_____

_____

_____

_____

_____

_____

_____

_____

_____

_____

_____

_____

As you consider the things you've written in the space above, ask yourself these questions:

Do I believe that a willingness to serve others is a sign of greatness in God's eyes?

Do I believe that I am surrounded by opportunities to serve and that I should take advantage of those opportunities?

BE AN ACTIVE PARTICIPANT IN GOD'S TRIUMPHANT CHURCH

And I also say to you that you are Peter, and on this rock I will build My church, and the forces of Hades will not overpower it. I will give you the keys of the kingdom of heaven, and whatever you bind on earth will have been bound in heaven, and whatever you loose on earth will have been loosed in heaven.

Matthew 16:18-19 Holman CSB

The Message

Jesus promised that the church would be triumphant. So, you simply can't go wrong investing your life in His church. The church is eternal.

The Bible teaches that we should worship God in our hearts and in our churches (Acts 20:28). We have clear instructions to "feed the church of God" and to worship our Creator in the presence of fellow believers.

We live in a world that is teeming with temptations and distractions—a world where good and evil struggle in a constant battle to win our minds, our hearts, and our souls. Our challenge, of course, is to ensure that we cast our lot on the side of God. One way that we remain faithful to Him is through the practice of regular, purposeful worship. When we worship the Father faithfully and fervently, we are blessed.

> The church is not an end in itself; it is a means to the end of the kingdom of God.
>
> *E. Stanley Jones*

The church belongs to God; it is His just as certainly as we are His. When we help build God's church, we bear witness to the changes that He has made in our lives.

Fellowship with other believers should be an integral part of your everyday life. Your association with fellow Christians should be uplifting, enlightening, encouraging, and consistent.

Are you an active member of your own fellowship? Are you a builder of bridges inside the four walls of your church and outside it? Do you contribute to God's glory by contributing your time and your talents to a close-knit band of believers? Hopefully so. The fellowship of believers is intended to be a powerful tool for spreading God's Good News and uplifting His children. And God intends for you to be a fully contributing member of that fellowship. Your intentions should be the same.

A LESSON TO THINK ABOUT

God wants you to be actively involved in His church.

53

WHAT GOD'S WORD SAYS ABOUT CHURCH

For we are God's fellow workers; you are God's field, you are God's building.

1 Corinthians 3:9 NKJV

Don't you realize that all of you together are the temple of God and that the Spirit of God lives in you?

1 Corinthians 3:16 NLT

Now you are the body of Christ, and members individually.

1 Corinthians 12:27 NKJV

Be on guard for yourselves and for all the flock, among which the Holy Spirit has made you overseers, to shepherd the church of God which He purchased with His own blood.

Acts 20:28 NASB

The church, you see, is not peripheral to the world; the world is peripheral to the church. The church is Christ's body, in which he speaks and acts, by which he fills everything with his presence.

Ephesians 1:23 MSG

WORDS OF WISDOM ABOUT CHURCH

Our churches are meant to be havens where the caste rules of the world do not apply.

Beth Moore

Be filled with the Holy Spirit; join a church where the members believe the Bible and know the Lord; seek the fellowship of other Christians; learn and be nourished by God's Word and His many promises. Conversion is not the end of your journey—it is only the beginning.

Corrie ten Boom

To model the kingdom of God in the world, the church must not only be a repentant community, committed to truth, but also a holy community.

Chuck Colson

Every time a new person comes to God, every time someone's gifts find expression in the fellowship of believers, every time a family in need is surrounded by the caring church, the truth is affirmed anew: the Church triumphant is alive and well!

Gloria Gaither

Notes to Yourself: _____

_____

_____

_____

_____

_____

_____

_____

_____

_____

_____

_____

_____

_____

As you consider the things you've written in the space above, ask yourself these questions:

Am I giving enough to my church—enough of my time, my talents, and my money?

Do I consider church a celebration or an obligation?

Do I view every worship service as an opportunity to praise God and enhance my own spiritual growth?

GOD'S WORD IS YOUR PROTECTION AGAINST TEMPTATION

But Jesus answered him, "It is written: Man must not live on bread alone." So he took Him up and showed Him all the kingdoms of the world in a moment of time. The Devil said to Him, "I will give You their splendor and all this authority, because it has been given over to me, and I can give it to anyone I want. If You, then, will worship me, all will be Yours." And Jesus answered him, "It is written: You shall worship the Lord your God, and Him alone you shall serve." So he took Him to Jerusalem, had Him stand on the pinnacle of the temple, and said to Him, "If You are the Son of God, throw Yourself down from here. . . ." And Jesus answered him, "It is said: You must not tempt the Lord your God."

Luke 4:4-12 Holman CSB

The Message

When the devil himself tried to tempt Jesus, Jesus used the Word of God as a defense against evil. So can we.

Because our world is filled with temptations, we confront them at every turn. Some of these temptations are small—eating a second piece of chocolate cake, for example. Too much cake may cause us to defile, at least in a modest way, the bodily temple that God has entrusted to our care. But two pieces of cake will not bring us to our knees. Other temptations, however, are not so harmless.

The devil, it seems, is working overtime these days, and causing heartache in more places and in more ways than ever before. We, as Christians, must remain vigilant. Not only must we resist Satan when he confronts us, but we must also avoid those places where Satan can most easily tempt us. And, if we are to avoid the unending temptations of this world, we must arm ourselves with the Word of God.

> It is easier to stay out of temptation than to get out of it.
>
> *Rick Warren*

In a letter to believers, Peter offered a stern warning: "Be sober, be vigilant; because your adversary the devil walks about like a roaring lion, seeking whom he may devour" (1 Peter 5:8 NKJV). What was true in New Testament times is equally true in our own. Satan tempts his prey and then devours them. And in these dangerous times, the tools that Satan uses to destroy his prey are more numerous than ever before.

As believing Christians, we must beware. And, if we seek righteousness in our own lives, we must earnestly wrap ourselves in the protection of God's Holy Word. After fasting forty days and nights in the desert, Jesus Himself was tempted by Satan. Christ used Scripture to rebuke the devil. We must do likewise. The Holy Bible provides us with a perfect blueprint for righteous living. If we consult that blueprint each day and follow its instructions carefully, we build our lives according to God's plan. And when we do, we are secure.

A LESSON TO THINK ABOUT

Because you live in a temptation-filled world, you must guard your eyes, your thoughts, and your heart—all day, every day.

WHAT GOD'S WORD SAYS ABOUT TEMPTATION

No temptation has overtaken you except what is common to humanity. God is faithful and He will not allow you to be tempted beyond what you are able, but with the temptation He will also provide a way of escape, so that you are able to bear it.

1 Corinthians 10:13 Holman CSB

Do not be deceived: "Bad company corrupts good morals."

1 Corinthians 15:33 Holman CSB

But the Lord is faithful; He will strengthen and guard you from the evil one.

2 Thessalonians 3:3 Holman CSB

The Lord knows how to deliver the godly out of temptations.

2 Peter 2:9 NKJV

Put on the full armor of God so that you can stand against the tactics of the Devil.

Ephesians 6:11 Holman CSB

Words of Wisdom About Temptation

Our battles are first won or lost in the secret places of our will in God's presence, never in full view of the world.

Oswald Chambers

A man who gives in to temptation after five minutes simply does not know what it would have been like an hour later.

C. S. Lewis

The only power the devil has is in getting people to believe his lies. If they don't believe his lies, he is powerless to get his work done.

Stormie Omartian

In the worst temptations nothing can help us but faith that God's Son has put on flesh, sits at the right hand of the Father, and prays for us. There is no mightier comfort.

Martin Luther

Notes to Yourself: _____

_____

_____

_____

_____

_____

_____

_____

_____

_____

_____

_____

_____

As you consider the things you've written in the space above, ask yourself these questions:

Am I fully aware that I live in a society brimming with temptations?

Do I avoid places where I might be tempted to disobey God?

Do I avoid people who might encourage me to compromise my beliefs or betray my conscience?

MATERIAL POSSESSIONS CAN BE VERY DANGEROUS

"For it is easier for a camel to go through the eye of a needle than for a rich person to enter the kingdom of God."
Those who heard this asked, "Then who can be saved?"
He replied, "What is impossible with men is possible with God."

Luke 18:25-27 Holman CSB

The Message

Jesus warned against the dangers of materialism, and we must take His warning seriously.

In our demanding world, financial prosperity can be a good thing, but spiritual prosperity is profoundly more important. Certainly we all need the basic necessities of life, but once we meet those needs for our families and ourselves, the piling up of possessions creates more problems than it solves. Our real riches, of course, are not of this world. We are never really rich until we are rich in spirit. Yet we live in a society that leads us to believe otherwise. The media often glorifies material possessions above all else; God most certainly does not.

> As faithful stewards of what we have, ought we not to give earnest thought to our staggering surplus?
>
> *Elisabeth Elliot*

Martin Luther observed, "Many things I have tried to grasp and have lost. That which I have placed in God's hands I still have." His words apply to all of us. Our earthly riches are transitory; our spiritual riches, on the other hand, are everlasting.

How much value do you place on your material possessions? And while you're pondering that question, ask yourself this: Do you own your possessions, or vice versa? If you don't like the answer you receive, make an ironclad promise to stop acquiring and start divesting.

Once you stop spending your hard-earned money on frivolous purchases, you'll be amazed at the things you can do without. You'll be pleasantly surprised at the sense of satisfaction that accompanies your newfound moderation. And you'll soon discover that when it comes to material possessions, less truly is more.

Do you find yourself wrapped up in the concerns of the material world? If so, it's time to reorder your priorities and reassess your values. And then, it's time to begin storing up riches that will endure throughout eternity—the spiritual kind.

A Lesson to Think About

Material possessions may seem appealing at first, but they pale in comparison to the spiritual gifts that God gives to those who put Him first. Count yourself among that number.

WHAT GOD'S WORD SAYS ABOUT MATERIALISM

For where your treasure is, there your heart will be also.

Luke 12:34 NKJV

He who trusts in his riches will fall, but the righteous will flourish . . . .

Proverbs 11:28 NKJV

No one can serve two masters. The person will hate one master and love the other, or will follow one master and refuse to follow the other. You cannot serve both God and worldly riches.

Matthew 6:24 NCV

A man's life does not consist in the abundance of his possessions.

Luke 12:15 NIV

Yes, a person is a fool to store up earthly wealth but not have a rich relationship with God.

Luke 12:21 NLT

WORDS OF WISDOM ABOUT MATERIALISM

Greed is enslaving. The more you have, the more you want—until eventually avarice consumes you.

Kay Arthur

The cross is laid on every Christian. It begins with the call to abandon the attachments of this world.

Dietrich Bonhoeffer

There is absolutely no evidence that complexity and materialism lead to happiness. On the contrary, there is plenty of evidence that simplicity and spirituality lead to joy, a blessedness that is better than happiness.

Dennis Swanberg

If you want to be truly happy, you won't find it on an endless quest for more stuff. You'll find it in receiving God's generosity and in then passing that generosity along.

Bill Hybels

Notes to Yourself: _____

_____

_____

_____

_____

_____

_____

_____

_____

_____

_____

_____

_____

As you consider the things you've written in the space above, ask yourself these questions:

Do I genuinely understand that material possessions will not bring me lasting happiness?

Do I understand that my possessions are actually God's possessions, and do I use those possessions for His purposes?

Do my spending habits reflect the values that I hold most dear, and am I a faithful steward of my resources?

LOVE YOUR NEIGHBORS, EVEN IF THEY'RE DIFFERENT

*A woman of Samaria came to draw water. "Give Me a drink,"
Jesus said to her, for His disciples had gone into town to buy food.
"How is it that You, a Jew, ask for a drink from me, a Samaritan
woman?" she asked. For Jews do not associate with Samaritans.
Jesus answered, "If you knew the gift of God, and who is saying
to you, 'Give Me a drink,' you would ask Him, and He would
give you living water." . . . Now many Samaritans from that
town believed in Him because of what the woman said when
she testified, "He told me everything I ever did."*

John 4:7-11, 39 Holman CSB

The Message

The woman at the well was so different from most of the
women Jesus encountered. She was a Samaritan, and she
had been divorced five times. Yet Jesus loved her and
validated her life.

There's an old saying that's both familiar and true: If you aren't really loving, you aren't really living. These words, like the familiar text of 1 Corinthians 13:13, remind us of the importance of love. Faith is important, of course. So too is hope. But love is more important still.

Love is a choice. Either you choose to behave lovingly toward others . . . or not; either you behave yourself in ways that enhance your relationships . . . or not. But make no mistake: genuine love requires effort. Simply put, if you wish to build lasting relationships, you must be willing to do your part.

Since the days of Adam and Eve, God has allowed His children to make choices for themselves, and so it is with you. As you interact with family and friends, you have choices to make—lots of choices. If you choose wisely, you'll be rewarded; if you choose unwisely, you'll bear the consequences.

> The truth of the Gospel is intended to free us to love God and others with our whole heart.
>
> *John Eldredge*

Christ's words are clear: we are to love God first, and secondly, we are to love others as we love ourselves (Matthew 22:37-40). These two commands are seldom easy, and because we are imperfect beings, we often fall short. But God's Holy Word commands us to try.

The Christian path is an exercise in love and forgiveness. If we are to walk in Christ's footsteps, we must forgive those who have done us harm, and we must accept Christ's love by sharing it freely with family, friends, neighbors, and even strangers.

God does not intend for you to experience mediocre relationships; He created you for far greater things. Building lasting relationships requires compassion, wisdom, empathy, kindness, courtesy, and forgiveness. If that sounds a lot like work, it is—which is perfectly fine with God. Why? Because He knows that you are capable of doing that work, and because He knows that the fruits of your labors will enrich the lives of your loved ones and the lives of generations yet unborn.

A LESSON TO THINK ABOUT

God is love, and He expects you to share His love with others.

WHAT GOD'S WORD SAYS ABOUT
LOVING OTHERS

And he has given us this command: Whoever loves God must also love his brother.

1 John 4:21 NIV

Jesus replied, "'Love the Lord your God with all your heart and with all your soul and with all your mind.' This is the first and greatest commandment. And the second is like it: 'Love your neighbor as yourself.' All the Law and the Prophets hang on these two commandments."

Matthew 22:37-40 NIV

And the Lord make you to increase and abound in love one toward another, and toward all men . . . .

1 Thessalonians 3:12 KJV

Above all, love each other deeply, because love covers over a multitude of sins.

1 Peter 4:8 NIV

Love one another deeply, from the heart.

1 Peter 1:22 NIV

Words of Wisdom About
Loving Others

If Jesus is the preeminent One in our lives, then we will love each other, submit to each other, and treat one another fairly in the Lord.

Warren Wiersbe

Beware that you are not swallowed up in books! An ounce of love is worth a pound of knowledge.

John Wesley

So Jesus came, stripping himself of everything as he came— omnipotence, omniscience, omnipresence—everything except love. "He emptied himself" (Philippians 2:7), emptied himself of everything except love. Love—his only protection, his only weapon, his only method.

E. Stanley Jones

The world does not understand theology or dogma, but it does understand love and sympathy.

D. L. Moody

Notes to Yourself: _____

_____

_____

_____

_____

_____

_____

_____

_____

_____

_____

_____

_____

As you consider the things you've written in the space above, ask yourself these questions:

Do I acknowledge that God is love, and that He wants me to love others?

Do I demonstrate my love for others through acts of kindness and generosity?

Am I usually courteous and patient with other people, and am I quick to forgive others?

WHEN CONFRONTING EVIL, DON'T BE NEUTRAL

*Then Jesus went into the temple of God and drove out
all those who bought and sold in the temple,
and overturned the tables of the money changers
and the seats of those who sold doves.*

Matthew 21:12 NKJV

The Message

God's Word condemns random anger; but Jesus
demonstrates that anger directed toward evil is justified.

Unbridled anger is counterproductive, and the Bible is filled with messages that warn us to control our tempers. But sometimes, anger can be a good thing. In the 21st chapter of Matthew, we are told how Christ responded when He confronted the evildoings of those who invaded His Father's house of worship. Jesus physically removed the profiteers from the temple. By doing so, He proved that righteous indignation is an appropriate response to evil.

We live in a society that encourages us to "look the other way" when we are confronted with evildoings. The world encourages us to view morality as a relative phenomenon, something that changes with societal trends. When we observe wrongdoing, we are encouraged to "live and let live." But God intends that we stand up for our beliefs, and He intends that we stand up for Him.

> *Discipline yourself for the purpose of godliness.*
> 1 Timothy 4:7 NASB

If you wish to build a life that is pleasing to your Creator, you should stand up to the temptations and distractions of modern-day society. Standing up for yourself—and for God—isn't always easy when so many

societal forces are struggling to compromise your character
. . . but with God's help, you can do it.

So, when you come face to face with the devil's
handiwork, don't be satisfied to remain safely on the
sidelines. Instead, follow in the footsteps of your Savior.
Jesus never compromised with evil, and neither should you.

A LESSON TO THINK ABOUT

Because God is just, He rewards good behavior just as
surely as He punishes sin. And there are no loopholes.

WHAT GOD'S WORD SAYS ABOUT RIGHTEOUSNESS

For the eyes of the Lord are on the righteous, and His ears are open to their prayers; but the face of the Lord is against those who do evil.

1 Peter 3:12 NKJV

Walk in a manner worthy of the God who calls you into His own kingdom and glory.

1 Thessalonians 2:12 NASB

Run away from infantile indulgence. Run after mature righteousness—faith, love, peace—joining those who are in honest and serious prayer before God.

2 Timothy 2:22 MSG

And you shall do what is right and good in the sight of the Lord, that it may be well with you.

Deuteronomy 6:18 NKJV

WORDS OF WISDOM ABOUT RIGHTEOUS ANGER

The greatest enemy of holiness is not passion; it is apathy.

John Eldredge

You have to say "yes" to God first before you can effectively say "no" to the devil.

Vance Havner

The first step on the way to victory is to recognize the enemy.

Corrie ten Boom

Christianity isn't a religion about going to Sunday school, potluck suppers, being nice, holding car washes, sending your secondhand clothes off to Mexico—as good as those things might be. This is a world at war.

John Eldredge

Sin must be destroyed, not corrected.

Oswald Chambers

Notes to Yourself: _____

_____

_____

_____

_____

_____

_____

_____

_____

_____

_____

_____

_____

_____

As you consider the things you've written in the space above, ask yourself these questions:

Am I aware that the potential for evil is inevitably woven into the fabric of human existence?

Am I willing to confront evil behavior, or am I more likely to ignore it?

Do I listen carefully to my conscience, and do I make sure that my actions are congruent with my beliefs?

DON'T BE TOO QUICK TO JUDGE OTHERS

Then the scribes and the Pharisees brought a woman caught in adultery, making her stand in the center. "Teacher," they said to Him, "this woman was caught in the act of committing adultery. In the law Moses commanded us to stone such women. So what do You say?" They asked this to trap Him, in order that they might have evidence to accuse Him. . . . He stood up and said to them, "The one without sin among you should be the first to throw a stone at her." Then He stooped down again and continued writing on the ground. When they heard this, they left one by one, starting with the older men. Only He was left, with the woman in the center. . . . "Neither do I condemn you," said Jesus. "Go, and from now on do not sin any more."

John 8:3-9, 11 Holman CSB

The Message

Jesus challenged the religious leaders of the day to cast stones only if they had never committed a sin. Then, He told the woman who had been caught in adultery to go and sin no more.

Even the most devoted Christians may fall prey to a powerful yet subtle temptation: the temptation to judge others. But as believers, we are commanded to refrain from such behavior. The warning of Matthew 7:1 is clear: "Judge not, that ye be not judged" (KJV).

Are you one of those people who finds it easy to judge others? If so, it's time to make radical changes in the way you view the world and the people who inhabit it.

When considering the shortcomings of others, you must remember this: in matters of judgment, God does not need (or want) your help. Why? Because God is perfectly capable of judging the human heart . . . while you are not. This message is made clear by the teachings of Jesus.

As Jesus came upon a young woman who had been condemned by the Pharisees, He spoke not only to the crowd that was gathered there, but also to all generations, when He warned, "He that is without sin among you, let him first cast a stone at her" (John 8:7 KJV).

> *Judge not, and ye shall not be judged: condemn not, and ye shall not be condemned . . . .*
> *Luke 6:37 KJV*

Christ's message is clear: because we are all sinners, we are commanded to refrain from judging others. Yet the irony is this: it precisely because we are sinners that we are so quick to judge.

All of us have all fallen short of God's laws, and none of us, therefore, are qualified to "cast the first stone." Thankfully, God has forgiven us, and we, too, must forgive others. Let us refrain, then, from judging our family members, our friends, and our loved ones. Instead, let us forgive them and love them in the same way that God has forgiven us.

A LESSON TO THINK ABOUT

To the extent you judge others, so, too, will you be judged. So you must, to the best of your ability, refrain from judgmental thoughts and words.

WHAT GOD'S WORD SAYS ABOUT JUDGING OTHERS

You, therefore, have no excuse, you who pass judgment on someone else, for at whatever point you judge the other, you are condemning yourself.

Romans 2:1 NIV

Speak and act as those who will be judged by the law of freedom. For judgment is without mercy to the one who hasn't shown mercy. Mercy triumphs over judgment.

James 2:12-13 Holman CSB

Do not judge, or you too will be judged. For in the same way you judge others, you will be judged, and with the measure you use, it will be measured to you.

Matthew 7:1 NIV

Why do you look at the speck of sawdust in your brother's eye and pay no attention to the plank in your own eye? How can you say to your brother, "Let me take the speck out of your eye," when all the time there is a plank in your own eye? You hypocrite, first take the plank out of your own eye, and then you will see clearly to remove the speck from your brother's eye.

Matthew 7:3-5 NIV

WORDS OF WISDOM ABOUT
JUDGING OTHERS; SECOND CHANCES

Christians think they are prosecuting attorneys or judges, when, in reality, God has called all of us to be witnesses.

Warren Wiersbe

Judging draws the judgment of others.

Catherine Marshall

Being critical of others, including God, is one way we try to avoid facing and judging our own sins.

Warren Wiersbe

Our Lord worked with people as they were, and He was patient—not tolerant of sin, but compassionate.

Vance Havner

Don't judge other people more harshly than you want God to judge you.

Marie T. Freeman

Notes to Yourself: _____

_____

_____

_____

_____

_____

_____

_____

_____

_____

_____

_____

As you consider the things you've written in the space above, ask yourself these questions:

Am I mindful that the Bible warns me not to judge others, and do I take that warning seriously?

When I catch myself being overly judgmental, do I try to stop myself and interrupt my critical thoughts before I become angry?

Do I find that when I am less judgmental, I improve the quality of my life?

BE COMPASSIONATE

Just as you want others to do for you,
do the same for them.

Luke 6:31 Holman CSB

The Message

Jesus was compassionate, and He commanded us to follow His example.

John Wesley's advice was straightforward: "Do all the good you can. By all the means you can. In all the ways you can. In all the places you can. At all the times you can. To all the people you can. As long as you can." One way to do all the good you can is to spread kindness wherever we go.

Sometimes, when we feel happy or generous, we find it easy to be compassionate. Other times, when we are discouraged or tired, we can scarcely summon the energy to utter a single kind word. But, God's commandment is clear: He intends that we make the conscious choice to treat others with kindness and respect, no matter our circumstances, no matter our emotions.

> *And let us be concerned about one another in order to promote love and good works.*
>
> Hebrews 10:24 Holman CSB

St. Teresa of Avila observed, "There are only two duties required of us—the love of God and the love of our neighbor, and the surest sign of discovering whether we observe these duties is the love of our neighbor." Her words remind us that we honor God by serving our friends and neighbors with kind words, heartfelt prayers, and helping hands. If we sincerely desire to follow in the footsteps of God's Son, we must make kindness and generosity the hallmark of our dealings with others.

Do you look for opportunities to share God's love with your family and friends? Hopefully you do. After all, your Heavenly Father has blessed you in countless ways, and He has instructed you to share your blessings with the world. So today, look for opportunities to spread kindness wherever you go. God deserves no less, and neither, for that matter, do your loved ones.

A LESSON TO THINK ABOUT

Compassionate words and deeds have echoes that last a lifetime and beyond.

WHAT GOD'S WORD SAYS ABOUT COMPASSION

Finally, all of you be of one mind, having compassion for one another; love as brothers, be tenderhearted, be courteous.

1 Peter 3:8 NKJV

Therefore, God's chosen ones, holy and loved, put on heartfelt compassion, kindness, humility, gentleness, and patience.

Colossians 3:12 Holman CSB

But he's already made it plain how to live, what to do, what God is looking for in men and women. It's quite simple: Do what is fair and just to your neighbor, be compassionate and loyal in your love, and don't take yourself too seriously—take God seriously.

Micah 6:8 MSG

I pray that your love for each other will overflow more and more, and that you will keep on growing in your knowledge and understanding.

Philippians 1:9 NLT

WORDS OF WISDOM ABOUT COMPASSION

When action-oriented compassion is absent, it's a tell-tale sign that something's spiritually amiss.

Bill Hybels

Our Lord worked with people as they were, and He was patient—not tolerant of sin, but compassionate.

Vance Havner

If we have the true love of God in our hearts, we will show it in our lives. We will not have to go up and down the earth proclaiming it. We will show it in everything we say or do.

D. L. Moody

When you launch an act of kindness out into the crosswinds of life, it will blow kindness back to you.

Dennis Swanberg

Kindness in this world will do much to help others, not only to come into the light, but also to grow in grace day by day.

Fanny Crosby

Notes to Yourself: _____

_____

_____

_____

_____

_____

_____

_____

_____

_____

_____

_____

_____

As you consider the things you've written in the space above, ask yourself these questions:

Do I sometimes allow myself to become so busy that I fail to observe the needs of my friends and family?

As a Christian, am I willing to apply the Golden Rule in every situation?

When I perform an act of kindness, do I avoid public acclaim?

REAL CHRISTIANITY REQUIRES OBEDIENCE TO GOD

Not everyone who says to Me, "Lord, Lord,"
shall enter the kingdom of heaven,
but he who does the will of My Father in heaven.

Matthew 7:21 NKJV

The Message

Jesus warns us that while many people may call His name, only those who obey God will follow in Christ's footsteps.

Obedience to God is determined, not by words, but by deeds. Talking about righteousness is easy; living righteously is far more difficult, especially in today's temptation-filled world.

Since God created Adam and Eve, we human beings have been rebelling against our Creator. Why? Because we are unwilling to trust God's Word, and we are unwilling to follow His commandments. God has given us a guidebook for righteous living called the Holy Bible. It contains thorough instructions which, if followed, lead to fulfillment, abundance, and salvation. But, if we choose to ignore God's commandments, the results are as predictable as they are tragic.

In Ephesians 2:10 we read, "For we are His workmanship, created in Christ Jesus for good works" (NKJV). These words are instructive: We are not saved by good works, but for good works. Good works are not the root, but rather the fruit of our salvation.

> *If they serve Him obediently, they will end their days in prosperity and their years in happiness.*
>
> Job 36:11 Holman CSB

When we seek righteousness in our own lives—and when we seek the companionship of those who do likewise—we reap the spiritual rewards that God intends for our lives. When we behave ourselves as godly men and women, we honor God. When we live righteously and according to God's commandments, He blesses us in ways that we cannot fully understand.

Do you seek God's peace and His blessings? Then obey Him. When you're faced with a difficult choice or a powerful temptation, seek God's counsel and trust the counsel He gives. Invite God into your heart and live according to His commandments. When you do, you will be blessed today and tomorrow and forever.

A LESSON TO THINK ABOUT

When you are obedient to God, you are secure; when you are not, you are not.

WHAT GOD'S WORD SAYS ABOUT OBEDIENCE

I have sought You with all my heart; don't let me wander from Your commands.

Psalm 119:10 Holman CSB

Therefore, everyone who hears these words of Mine and acts on them will be like a sensible man who built his house on the rock. The rain fell, the rivers rose, and the winds blew and pounded that house. Yet it didn't collapse, because its foundation was on the rock.

Matthew 7:24–25 Holman CSB

Just then someone came up and asked Him, "Teacher, what good must I do to have eternal life?" "Why do you ask Me about what is good?" He said to him. "There is only One who is good. If you want to enter into life, keep the commandments."

Matthew 19:16-17 Holman CSB

Jesus answered, "If anyone loves Me, he will keep My word. My Father will love him, and We will come to him and make Our home with him.

John 14:23 Holman CSB

WORDS OF WISDOM ABOUT OBEDIENCE

True faith commits us to obedience.

A. W. Tozer

Let us never suppose that obedience is impossible or that holiness is meant only for a select few. Our Shepherd leads us in paths of righteousness—not for our name's sake but for His.

Elisabeth Elliot

When you suffer and lose, that does not mean you are being disobedient to God. In fact, it might mean you're right in the center of His will. The path of obedience is often marked by times of suffering and loss.

Charles Swindoll

Trials and sufferings teach us to obey the Lord by faith, and we soon learn that obedience pays off in joyful ways.

Bill Bright

Obedience is the road to freedom, humility the road to pleasure, unity the road to personality.

C. S. Lewis

Notes to Yourself: _____

_____

_____

_____

_____

_____

_____

_____

_____

_____

_____

_____

As you consider the things you've written in the space above, ask yourself these questions:

Am I willing to study God's Word seriously and consistently?

Will I strive to obey God's commandments?

Will I associate with fellow believers who, by their words and actions, encourage me to obey God?

MIRACLES HAPPEN

*And immediately Jesus stretched out His hand
and caught him, and said to him,
"O you of little faith, why did you doubt?"*

Matthew 14:31 NKJV

The Message

To do miraculous things, you need faith. To do the impossible, you must stay focused on Jesus and have faith in Him.

Jesus performed many miracles, and we still live in a world where miracles are taking place all around us. But sometimes, because of limited faith and limited understanding, we wrongly assume that God cannot or will not intervene in the affairs of mankind. Such assumptions are simply wrong.

Are you afraid to ask God to do big things in your life? Is your faith threadbare and worn? If so, it's time to abandon your doubts and reclaim your faith—faith in yourself, faith in your abilities, faith in your future, and faith in your Heavenly Father.

> *For nothing will be impossible with God.*
> Luke 1:37 Holman CSB

Catherine Marshall notes that, "God specializes in things thought impossible." And make no mistake: God can help you do things you never dreamed possible . . . your job is to let Him.

Sometimes, when we read of God's miraculous works in Biblical times, we tell ourselves, "That was then, but this is now." When we do so, we are mistaken. God is with His children "now" just as He was "then." He is right here, right now, performing miracles. And, He will continue to work miracles in our lives to the extent we are willing to trust in Him and to the extent those miracles fit into the fabric of His divine plan.

Miracles—both great and small—happen around us all day every day, but usually, we're too busy to notice. Some miracles, like the twinkling of a star or the glory of a sunset, we take for granted. Other miracles, like the healing of a terminally sick patient, we chalk up to fate or to luck. We assume, quite incorrectly, that God is "out there" and we are "right here." Nothing could be farther from the truth.

Do you lack the faith that God can work miracles in your own life? If so, it's time to reconsider. Instead of doubting God, trust His power, and expect His miracles. Then, wait patiently . . . because something miraculous is about to happen.

A LESSON TO THINK ABOUT

God does miraculous things, so you should never be afraid to ask Him to perform a miracle.

WHAT GOD'S WORD SAYS ABOUT MIRACLES

Looking at them, Jesus said, "With men it is impossible, but not with God, because all things are possible with God."

Mark 10:27 Holman CSB

I assure you: The one who believes in Me will also do the works that I do. And he will do even greater works than these, because I am going to the Father.

John 14:12 Holman CSB

But as it is written: "Eye has not seen, nor ear heard, nor have entered into the heart of man the things which God has prepared for those who love Him."

1 Corinthians 2:9 NKJV

You are the God who works wonders; You revealed Your strength among the peoples.

Psalm 77:14 Holman CSB

WORDS OF WISDOM ABOUT MIRACLES

The miracles in fact are a retelling in small letters of the very same story which is written across the whole world in letters too large for some of us to see.

C. S. Lewis

When God is involved, anything can happen. Be open and stay that way. God has a beautiful way of bringing good vibrations out of broken chords.

Charles Swindoll

When we face an impossible situation, all self-reliance and self-confidence must melt away; we must be totally dependent on Him for the resources.

Anne Graham Lotz

Only God can move mountains, but faith and prayer can move God.

E. M. Bounds

God specializes in things thought impossible.

Catherine Marshall

Notes to Yourself: _____

_____

_____

_____

_____

_____

_____

_____

_____

_____

_____

_____

_____

As you consider the things you've written in the space above, ask yourself these questions:

Do I believe that God can do miraculous things?

Do I remain watchful for miracles both large and small?

Do I believe that all things are possible for those who believe, or am I living under a cloud of pessimism and doubt?

FORGIVENESS IS NOT OPTIONAL

Then Jesus said, "Father, forgive them,
for they do not know what they do."
And they divided His garments and cast lots.

Luke 23:34 NKJV

The Message

Even while He endured the pain of the crucifixion, Jesus would not withhold forgiveness from the men who were killing Him. Jesus was—and is—a model of forgiveness.

It has been said that life is an exercise in forgiveness. How true. Christ understood the importance of forgiveness when He commanded, "Love your enemies and pray for those who persecute you" (Matthew 5:43-44 NIV). But sometimes, forgiveness is difficult indeed.

When we have been injured or embarrassed, we feel the urge to strike back and to hurt the ones who have hurt us. But Christ instructs us to do otherwise. Christ teaches us that forgiveness is God's way and that mercy is an integral part of God's plan for our lives. In short, we are commanded to weave the thread of forgiveness into the very fabric of our lives.

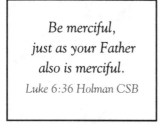

*Be merciful,
just as your Father
also is merciful.*
Luke 6:36 Holman CSB

Do you invest more time than you should reliving the past? Are you troubled by feelings of anger, bitterness, envy, or regret? Do you harbor ill will against someone whom you simply can't seem to forgive? If so, it's time to finally get serious about forgiveness.

When someone hurts you, the act of forgiveness is difficult, but necessary. Until you forgive, you are trapped in a prison of your own creation. But what if you have tried to forgive and simply can't seem to do so? The solution to your dilemma is this: you simply must make forgiveness a higher priority in your life.

Most of us don't spend too much time thinking about forgiveness; we worry, instead, about the injustices we have suffered and the people who inflicted them. God has a better plan: He wants us to live in the present, not the past, and He knows that in order to do so, we must forgive those who have harmed us.

Have you made forgiveness a high priority? Have you sincerely asked God to forgive you for your inability to forgive others? Have you genuinely prayed that those feelings of hatred and anger might be swept from your heart? If so, congratulations. If not, perhaps it's time to rearrange your priorities . . . and perhaps it's time to free yourself from the chains of bitterness and regret.

A LESSON TO THINK ABOUT

God's Word instructs you to forgive others . . . no exceptions.

WHAT GOD'S WORD SAYS ABOUT FORGIVENESS

All bitterness, anger and wrath, insult and slander must be removed from you, along with all wickedness. And be kind and compassionate to one another, forgiving one another, just as God also forgave you in Christ.

Ephesians 4:31-32 Holman CSB

See to it that no one repays evil for evil to anyone, but always pursue what is good for one another and for all.

1 Thessalonians 5:15 Holman CSB

A person's insight gives him patience, and his virtue is to overlook an offense.

Proverbs 19:11 Holman CSB

And forgive us our sins, for we ourselves also forgive everyone in debt to us.

Luke 11:4 Holman CSB

WORDS OF WISDOM ABOUT FORGIVENESS

As you have received the mercy of God by the forgiveness of sin and the promise of eternal life, thus you must show mercy.

Billy Graham

Only the truly forgiven are truly forgiving.

C. S. Lewis

Our relationships with other people are of primary importance to God. Because God is love, He cannot tolerate any unforgiveness or hardness in us toward any individual.

Catherine Marshall

Forgiveness is not an emotion. Forgiveness is an act of the will, and the will can function regardless of the temperature of the heart.

Corrie ten Boom

Revenge is the raging fire that consumes the arsonist.

Max Lucado

Notes to Yourself: _____

_____

_____

_____

_____

_____

_____

_____

_____

_____

_____

As you consider the things you've written in the space above, ask yourself these questions:

Am I willing to acknowledge the important role that forgiveness should play in my life?

Will I strive to forgive those who have hurt me, even when doing so is difficult?

Do I understand that forgiveness is a marathon (not a sprint), and will I prayerfully ask God to help me move beyond the emotions of bitterness and regret?

BUILD A LOVING RELATIONSHIP WITH JESUS

*So when they had eaten breakfast, Jesus said to Simon Peter,
"Simon, son of Jonah, do you love Me more than these?"
He said to Him, "Yes, Lord; You know that I love You." He said
to him, "Feed My lambs." He said to him again a second time,
"Simon, son of Jonah, do you love Me?" He said to Him,
"Yes, Lord; You know that I love You." He said to him,
"Tend My sheep." He said to him the third time, "Simon, son
of Jonah, do you love Me?" Peter was grieved because He said
to him the third time, "Do you love Me?" And he said to Him,
"Lord, You know all things; You know that I love You."
Jesus said to him, "Feed My sheep."*

John 21:15-17 NKJV

The Message

Three times Jesus inquired of Peter, "Do you love Me?"
Thus did the Master emphasize the need for His followers
to build a loving relationship with Him.

Jesus loved you so much that He endured unspeakable humiliation and suffering for you. How will you respond to Christ's sacrifice? Will you take up His cross and follow Him (Luke 9:23), or will you choose another path? When you place your hopes squarely at the foot of the cross, when you place Jesus squarely at the center of your life, you will be blessed. When you build a growing, loving relationship with the One from Galilee, your life will be changed now and forever.

The 19th-century writer Hannah Whitall Smith observed, "The crucial question for each of us is this: What do you think of Jesus, and do you yet have a personal acquaintance with Him?" Indeed, the answer to that question determines the quality, the course, and the direction of our lives today and for all eternity.

> The key to my understanding of the Bible is a personal relationship to Jesus Christ.
>
> *Oswald Chambers*

The old familiar hymn begins, "What a friend we have in Jesus." No truer words were ever penned. Jesus is the sovereign Friend and ultimate Savior of mankind. Christ showed enduring love for His believers by willingly sacrificing His own life so that we might have eternal life. Now, it is our turn to become His friend.

Let us love our Savior, praise Him, and share His message of salvation with our neighbors and with the world. When we do, we demonstrate that our acquaintance with the Master is not a passing fancy; it is, instead, the cornerstone and the touchstone of our lives.

A LESSON TO THINK ABOUT

Jesus loves you, and you, in turn, should love Him. Christ's love can—and should—be the cornerstone and the touchstone of your life.

WHAT GOD'S WORD SAYS ABOUT LOVING JESUS

And Jesus said to them, "I am the bread of life. He who comes to Me shall never hunger, and he who believes in Me shall never thirst."

John 6:35 NKJV

Greater love has no one than this, than to lay down one's life for his friends.

John 15:13 NKJV

If you love me, you will obey what I command.

John 14:15 NIV

And we know that in all things God works for the good of those who love him, who have been called according to his purpose.

Romans 8:28 NIV

Just as the Father has loved Me, I have also loved you; abide in My love.

John 15:9 NASB

WORDS OF WISDOM ABOUT
LOVING JESUS

Jesus be mine forever, my God, my heaven, my all.

C. H. Spurgeon

Tell me the story of Jesus. Write on my heart every word.
Tell me the story most precious, sweetest that ever was
heard.

Fanny Crosby

I am truly happy with Jesus Christ. I couldn't live without
Him. When my life gets beyond the ability to cope, He takes
over.

Ruth Bell Graham

Jesus Christ is the first and last, author and finisher,
beginning and end, alpha and omega, and by Him all other
things hold together. He must be first or nothing. God never
comes next!

Vance Havner

Notes to Yourself: _____

_____

_____

_____

_____

_____

_____

_____

_____

_____

_____

_____

_____

As you consider the things you've written in the space above, ask yourself these questions:

Do I believe that Jesus gave His life so that I might have eternal life?

Do I genuinely love Christ, and have I made Him the cornerstone of my life?

Am I willing to talk about the role that Jesus plays in my life, or do I usually keep my feelings to myself?

GIVE SACRIFICIALLY

*So He called His disciples to Himself and said to them,
"Assuredly, I say to you that this poor widow has put in more
than all those who have given to the treasury;
for they all put in out of their abundance, but she out of her
poverty put in all that she had, her whole livelihood."*

Mark 12:43-44 NKJV

The Message

Jesus told His disciples a parable about a poor widow
who gave all she had as an offering to God. Thus Jesus
encouraged His followers to give sacrificially.

The parable about the widow who gave all she had was Jesus' way of teaching His disciples to give sacrificially. In Matthew 10:8, Christ reinforced this message: "Freely you have received, freely give" (NIV). And, of course, Christ's words still apply—as believers, we are commanded to be generous with our friends, with our families, and with those in need. We must give freely of our time, our possessions, and, most especially, our love.

Christ showed His love for us by willingly sacrificing His own life so that we might have eternal life: "But God demonstrates His own love for us in this: While we were still sinners, Christ died for us" (Romans 5:8 NIV). We, as Christ's followers, are challenged to share His love. And, when we walk each day with Jesus—and obey the commandments found in God's Holy Word—we are worthy ambassadors for Him. Just as Christ has been—and will always be—the ultimate friend to His flock, so should we be Christlike in our love and generosity to those in need. When we share the love of Christ, we share a priceless gift. As His servants, we must do no less.

> Let us give according to our incomes, lest God make our incomes match our gifts.
> *Peter Marshall*

So today, take God's words to heart and make this pledge: Be a cheerful, generous, courageous giver. The world needs your help, and you need the spiritual rewards that will be yours when you give it.

A LESSON TO THINK ABOUT

God has given you countless blessings . . . and He wants you to share them.

WHAT GOD'S WORD SAYS ABOUT GIVING

So let each one give as he purposes in his heart, not grudgingly or of necessity; for God loves a cheerful giver.

2 Corinthians 9:7 NKJV

Dear friend, you are showing your faith by whatever you do for the brothers, and this you are doing for strangers.

3 John 1:5 Holman CSB

In every way I've shown you that by laboring like this, it is necessary to help the weak and to keep in mind the words of the Lord Jesus, for He said, "It is more blessed to give than to receive."

Acts 20:35 Holman CSB

Bear one another's burdens, and so fulfill the law of Christ.

Galatians 6:2 NKJV

If a brother or sister is without clothes and lacks daily food, and one of you says to them, "Go in peace, keep warm, and eat well," but you don't give them what the body needs, what good is it?

James 2:15–16 Holman CSB

WORDS OF WISDOM ABOUT GIVING

I can usually sense that a leading is from the Holy Spirit when it calls me to humble myself, to serve somebody, to encourage somebody, or to give something away. Very rarely will the evil one lead us to do those kind of things.

Bill Hybels

Jesus had a loving heart. If he dwells within us, hatred and bitterness will never rule us.

Billy Graham

God does not supply money to satisfy our every whim and desire. His promise is to meet our needs and provide an abundance so that we can help other people.

Larry Burkett

For many of us, the great obstacle to charity lies not in our luxurious living or desire for more money, but in our fear of insecurity.

C. S. Lewis

Notes to Yourself: _____

_____

_____

_____

_____

_____

_____

_____

_____

_____

_____

As you consider the things you've written in the space above, ask yourself these questions:

When I have questions about the level of my giving, am I willing to ask God for guidance?

Do I clearly understand that God has commanded me to be generous?

Do I believe that when I obey God's commandments, that I will be blessed because of my obedience?

LET YOUR LIGHT SHINE BRIGHTLY

Then Jesus spoke to them again:
"I am the light of the world. Anyone who follows Me will never
walk in the darkness, but will have the light of life."

John 8:12 Holman CSB

The Message

Jesus instructed His followers to walk in the light and, by doing so, become powerful examples to the world. And the same instructions apply to us: we must walk—and live—in the light, not the darkness.

Whether we like it or not, all of us are role models. Our friends and family members watch our actions and, as followers of Christ, we are obliged to act accordingly.

What kind of example are you? Are you the kind of person whose life serves as a genuine example of righteousness? Does your behavior serve as a positive role model for others? Are you the kind of believer whose actions, day in and day out, are based upon kindness, faithfulness, and a love for the Lord? If so, you are not only blessed by God, but you are also a powerful force for good in a world that desperately needs positive influences such as yours.

> *Set an example of good works yourself, with integrity and dignity in your teaching.*
> Titus 2:7 Holman CSB

Phillips Brooks had simple advice for believers of every generation; he said, "Be such a person, and live such a life, that if every person were such as you, and every life a life like yours, this earth would be God's Paradise." And that's precisely the kind of Christian you should strive to be . . . but it isn't always easy.

You live in a dangerous, temptation-filled world. That's why you encounter so many opportunities to stray from

God's commandments. Resist those temptations! When you do, you'll earn God's blessings, and you'll serve as a positive role model for your family and friends.

Corrie ten Boom advised, "Don't worry about what you do not understand. Worry about what you do understand in the Bible but do not live by." And that's sound advice because your families and friends are watching . . . and so, for that matter, is God.

A LESSON TO THINK ABOUT

God wants you to be a good example to your family, to your friends, and to the world.

WHAT GOD'S WORD SAYS ABOUT EXAMPLE

You should be an example to the believers in speech, in conduct, in love, in faith, in purity.

1 Timothy 4:12 Holman CSB

Do everything without grumbling and arguing, so that you may be blameless and pure.

Philippians 2:14–15 Holman CSB

For the kingdom of God is not in talk but in power.

1 Corinthians 4:20 Holman CSB

Therefore since we also have such a large cloud of witnesses surrounding us, let us lay aside every weight and the sin that so easily ensnares us, and run with endurance the race that lies before us.

Hebrews 12:1 Holman CSB

WORDS OF WISDOM ABOUT EXAMPLE

Integrity of heart is indispensable.

John Calvin

If I take care of my character, my reputation will take care of itself.

D. L. Moody

There is no way to grow a saint overnight. Character, like the oak tree, does not spring up like a mushroom.

Vance Havner

Your light is the truth of the Gospel message itself as well as your witness as to who Jesus is and what He has done for you. Don't hide it.

Anne Graham Lotz

You can never separate a leader's actions from his character.

John Maxwell

Notes to Yourself: _____

_____

_____

_____

_____

_____

_____

_____

_____

_____

_____

_____

_____

As you consider the things you've written in the space above, ask yourself these questions:

Do I always think about the way that my behavior will impact family and friends?

Do my actions follow along with my beliefs?

Am I fully aware of the messages that my behavior sends to others?

BE HUMBLE

Let this mind be in you which was also in Christ Jesus, who, being in the form of God, did not consider it robbery to be equal with God, but made Himself of no reputation, taking the form of a bondservant, and coming in the likeness of men. And being found in appearance as a man, He humbled Himself and became obedient to the point of death, even the death of the cross.

Philippians 2:5-8 NKJV

The Message

Jesus showed humility when He came from heaven and took on the role of servant. And as we consider Christ's sacrifice, we, too, must be humble.

Are you a humble believer who always gives credit where credit is due? If so, you are both wise and blessed.

Dietrich Bonhoeffer observed, "It is very easy to overestimate the importance of our own achievements in comparison with what we owe others." How true. Even those of us who consider ourselves "self-made" men and women are deeply indebted to more people than we can count. Our first and greatest indebtedness, of course, is to God and His only begotten Son. But we are also indebted to ancestors, parents, teachers, friends, spouses, family members, coworkers, fellow believers . . . and the list goes on.

> *God is against the proud, but he gives grace to the humble.*
> 1 Peter 5:5 NCV

With so many people who rightfully deserve to share the credit for our successes, how can we gloat? The answer, of course, is that we should not. But we inhabit a world in which far too many of our role models are remarkably haughty and surprisingly self-centered (hopefully, these are not your role models).

The Bible contains stern warnings against the sin of pride. One such warning is found in Proverbs 16:8: "Pride goes before destruction, and a haughty spirit before a fall" (NKJV). God's Word makes it clear: pride and destruction are traveling companions (but hopefully, they're not your traveling companions).

Jonathan Edwards observed, "Nothing sets a person so much out of the devil's reach as humility." So, if you're celebrating a worthwhile accomplishment, don't invite the devil to celebrate with you. Instead of puffing out your chest and saying, "Look at me!", give credit where credit is due, starting with God. And rest assured: There is no such thing as a self-made man. All of us are made by God . . . and He deserves the glory, not us.

A LESSON TO THINK ABOUT

God favors the humble just as surely as He disciplines the proud. You must remain humble or face the consequences.

WHAT GOD'S WORD SAYS ABOUT HUMILITY

Finally, all of you should be of one mind, full of sympathy toward each other, loving one another with tender hearts and humble minds.

1 Peter 3:8 NLT

Therefore humble yourselves under the mighty hand of God, that He may exalt you at the proper time, casting all your anxiety on Him, because He cares for you.

1 Peter 5:6-7 NASB

If My people who are called by My name will humble themselves, and pray and seek My face, and turn from their wicked ways, then I will hear from heaven, and will forgive their sin and heal their land.

2 Chronicles 7:14 NKJV

God has chosen you and made you his holy people. He loves you. So always do these things: Show mercy to others, be kind, humble, gentle, and patient.

Colossians 3:12 NCV

WORDS OF WISDOM ABOUT HUMILITY

Jesus had a humble heart. If He abides in us, pride will never dominate our lives.

Billy Graham

Humility is the fairest and rarest flower that blooms.

Charles Swindoll

That's what I love about serving God. In His eyes, there are no little people . . . because there are no big people. We are all on the same playing field. We all start at square one. No one has it better than the other, or possesses unfair advantage.

Joni Eareckson Tada

All kindness and good deeds, we must keep silent. The result will be an inner reservoir of personality power.

Catherine Marshall

Let the love of Christ be believed in and felt in your hearts, and it will humble you.

C. H. Spurgeon

Notes to Yourself: _____

_____

_____

_____

_____

_____

_____

_____

_____

_____

_____

_____

_____

As you consider the things you've written in the space above, ask yourself these questions:

Do I humbly acknowledge God's blessings every day?

Will I gratefully acknowledge those people who have helped me accomplish my goals?

Do I strive to give credit where credit is due . . . starting with God?

YOU CAN FIND JOY IN CHRIST

*I have spoken these things to you so that
My joy may be in you and your joy may be complete.*

John 15:11 Holman CSB

The Message

Joy is found in Jesus—knowing Him, loving Him, and serving Him. He is the vine, and we are the branches.

Have you made the choice to rejoice? If you're a Christian, you have every reason to be joyful. After all, the ultimate battle has already been won on the cross at Calvary. And if your life has been transformed by Christ's sacrifice, then you, as a recipient of God's grace, have every reason to live joyfully. Yet sometimes, amid the inevitable hustle and bustle of life here on earth, you may lose sight of your blessings as you wrestle with the challenges of everyday life.

Do you seek happiness, abundance, and contentment? If so, here are some things you should do: Love God and His Son; depend upon God for strength; try, to the best of your abilities, to follow God's will; and strive to obey His Holy Word. When you do these things, you'll discover that happiness goes hand-in-hand with righteousness. The happiest people are not those who rebel against God; the happiest people are those who love God and obey His commandments.

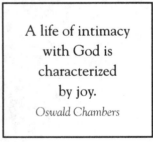

A life of intimacy with God is characterized by joy.

Oswald Chambers

What does life have in store for you? A world full of possibilities (of course it's up to you to seize them) and God's promise of abundance (of course it's up to you to accept it). So, as you embark upon the next phase of your journey, remember to celebrate the life that God has given you. Your Creator has blessed you beyond measure. Honor Him with your prayers, your words, your deeds, and your joy.

A LESSON TO THINK ABOUT

Joy begins with a choice—the choice to establish a genuine relationship with God and His Son. Joy does not depend upon your circumstances, but upon your relationship with God.

WHAT GOD'S WORD SAYS ABOUT
JOY

Weeping may spend the night, but there is joy in the morning.

Psalm 30:5 Holman CSB

A joyful heart is good medicine, but a broken spirit dries up the bones.

Proverbs 17:22 NASB

Always be full of joy in the Lord. I say it again—rejoice!

Philippians 4:4 NLT

Rejoice, and be exceeding glad: for great is your reward in heaven . . . .

Matthew 5:12 KJV

Shout for joy to the LORD, all the earth. Worship the LORD with gladness; come before him with joyful songs.

Psalm 100:1-2 NIV

Words of Wisdom About
Joy

Joy is the direct result of having God's perspective on our daily lives and the effect of loving our Lord enough to obey His commands and trust His promises.

Bill Bright

Our sense of joy, satisfaction, and fulfillment in life increases, no matter what the circumstances, if we are in the center of God's will.

Billy Graham

Joy is the heart's harmonious response to the Lord's song of love.

A. W. Tozer

Rejoice, the Lord is King; Your Lord and King adore!
Rejoice, give thanks and sing and triumph evermore.

Charles Wesley

Notes to Yourself: _____

_____

_____

_____

_____

_____

_____

_____

_____

_____

_____

_____

_____

_____

As you consider the things you've written in the space above, ask yourself these questions:

Do I try to treat each day as a cause for celebration?

Do I praise God many times each day?

Am I willing to share my enthusiasm with family, with friends, and with the world?

YOU CAN TAP IN TO GOD'S POWER

*But you will receive power when the Holy Spirit
has come upon you, and you will be My witnesses in Jerusalem,
in all Judea and Samaria, and to the ends of the earth.*

Acts 1:8 Holman CSB

The Message

Jesus promised that He would give us the strength to do
His work. Our task is to accept God's power and use it for
His kingdom.

Even the most inspired Christians can, from time to time, find themselves running on empty. The demands of daily life can drain us of our strength and rob us of the joy that is rightfully ours in Christ. When we find ourselves tired, discouraged, or worse, there is a source from which we can draw the power needed to recharge our spiritual batteries. That source is God.

God intends that His children lead joyous lives filled with abundance and peace. But sometimes, abundance and peace seem very far away. It is then that we must turn to God for renewal, and when we do, He will restore us if we allow Him to do so.

> When we spend time with Christ, He supplies us with strength and encourages us in the pursuit of His ways.
>
> *Elizabeth George*

Today, like every other day, is literally brimming with possibilities. Whether we realize it or not, God is always working in us and through us; our job is to let Him do His work without undue interference. Yet we are imperfect beings who, because of our limited vision, often resist God's will. And oftentimes, because of our stubborn insistence on squeezing too many activities into a 24-hour day, we allow ourselves to become exhausted or frustrated, or both.

Are you tired or troubled? Turn your heart toward God in prayer. Are you weak or worried? Take the time—or, more accurately, make the time—to delve deeply into God's Holy Word. Are you spiritually depleted? Call upon fellow believers to support you, and call upon Christ to renew your spirit and your life. Are you simply overwhelmed by the demands of the day? Pray for the wisdom to simplify your life. Are you exhausted? Pray for the wisdom to rest a little more and worry a little less.

When you do these things, you'll discover that the Creator of the universe stands always ready and always able to create a new sense of wonderment and joy in you.

A LESSON TO THINK ABOUT

When you are tired, fearful, or discouraged, God can restore your strength.

WHAT GOD'S WORD SAYS ABOUT STRENGTH

And He said to me, "My grace is sufficient for you, for My strength is made perfect in weakness."

2 Corinthians 12:9 NKJV

You, therefore, my child, be strong in the grace that is in Christ Jesus.

2 Timothy 2:1 Holman CSB

The Lord is my strength and my song; He has become my salvation.

Exodus 15:2 Holman CSB

He gives strength to the weary and strengthens the powerless.

Isaiah 40:29 Holman CSB

Finally, be strengthened by the Lord and by His vast strength.

Ephesians 6:10 Holman CSB

WORDS OF WISDOM ABOUT STRENGTH

No matter how heavy the burden, daily strength is given, so I expect we need not give ourselves any concern as to what the outcome will be. We must simply go forward.

Annie Armstrong

God conquers only what we yield to Him. Yet, when He does, and when our surrender is complete, He fills us with a new strength that we could never have known by ourselves. His conquest is our victory!

Shirley Dobson

A divine strength is given to those who yield themselves to the Father and obey what He tells them to do.

Warren Wiersbe

If we take God's program, we can have God's power—not otherwise.

E. Stanley Jones

Notes to Yourself: _____

_____

_____

_____

_____

_____

_____

_____

_____

_____

_____

_____

As you consider the things you've written in the space above, ask yourself these questions:

Do I gain strength and courage when I allow Christ to dwell in the center of my heart?

Do I gain strength through prayer?

Do I understand the importance of regular exercise and sensible rest?

BE LOYAL
TO GOD

"Follow Me," Jesus told them,
"and I will make you into fishers of men!"
Immediately they left their nets and followed Him.

Mark 1:17-18 Holman CSB

The Message

Christ's instructions were clear: His disciples were to give
Him their undivided loyalty. And so must we.

When Jesus addressed His disciples, He warned that each one must "take up his cross and follow me." The disciples must have known exactly what the Master meant. In Jesus' day, prisoners were forced to carry their own crosses to the location where they would be put to death. Thus, Christ's message was clear: in order to follow Him, Christ's disciples must deny themselves and, instead, trust Him completely. Nothing has changed since then.

If we are to be disciples of Christ, we must trust Him and place Him at the very center of our beings. Jesus never comes "next." He is always first. The paradox, of course, is that only by sacrificing ourselves to Him do we gain salvation for ourselves.

> *Be imitators of God,*
> *therefore,*
> *as dearly loved children.*
> Ephesians 5:1 NIV

The 19th-century writer Hannah Whitall Smith observed, "The crucial question for each of us is this: What do you think of Jesus, and do you yet have a personal acquaintance with Him?" Indeed, the answer to that question will determine the quality, the course, and the direction of your life today and for all eternity.

Jesus has called upon believers of every generation (and that includes you) to walk with Him. Jesus promises that when you follow in His footsteps, He will teach you how to live freely and lightly (Matthew 11:28-30). And when Jesus makes a promise, you can depend upon it.

Are you worried or anxious? Be confident in the power of Christ. He will never desert you. Are you discouraged? Be courageous and call upon your Savior. He will protect you and use you according to His purposes. Do you seek to be a worthy disciple of the One from Galilee? Then pick up His cross today and every day of your life. When you do, He will bless you now . . . and forever.

A LESSON TO THINK ABOUT

Jesus has invited you to become His disciple. If you accept His invitation—and if you obey His commandments—you will be protected and blessed.

WHAT GOD'S WORD SAYS ABOUT DISCIPLESHIP

You did not choose Me, but I chose you. I appointed you that you should go out and produce fruit, and that your fruit should remain, so that whatever you ask the Father in My name, He will give you.

John 15:16 Holman CSB

But whoever keeps His word, truly in him the love of God is perfected. This is how we know we are in Him: the one who says he remains in Him should walk just as He walked.

1 John 2:5-6 Holman CSB

We encouraged, comforted, and implored each one of you to walk worthy of God, who calls you into His own kingdom and glory.

1 Thessalonians 2:12 Holman CSB

The one who loves his life will lose it, and the one who hates his life in this world will keep it for eternal life. If anyone serves Me, he must follow Me. Where I am, there My servant also will be. If anyone serves Me, the Father will honor him.

John 12:25-26 Holman CSB

WORDS OF WISDOM ABOUT DISCIPLESHIP

In our faith we follow in someone's steps. In our faith we leave footprints to guide others. It's the principle of discipleship.

Max Lucado

A disciple is a follower of Christ. That means you take on His priorities as your own. His agenda becomes your agenda. His mission becomes your mission.

Charles Stanley

As we seek to become disciples of Jesus Christ, we should never forget that the word *disciple* is directly related to the word *discipline*. To be a disciple of the Lord Jesus Christ is to know His discipline.

Dennis Swanberg

A follower is never greater than his leader; a follower never draws attention to himself.

Franklin Graham

Notes to Yourself: _____

_____

_____

_____

_____

_____

_____

_____

_____

_____

_____

_____

_____

_____

As you consider the things you've written in the space above, ask yourself these questions:

Am I confident that my relationship with Jesus is as strong as it should be?

Am I experiencing the joyful abundance that is promised in John 10:10?

Am I able to resist the temptations and distractions of the world as I follow in Christ's footsteps?

YOU CAN FIND PEACE

Peace I leave with you. My peace I give to you.
I do not give to you as the world gives.
Your heart must not be troubled or fearful.

John 14:27 Holman CSB

The Message

Jesus can quiet the storms of life—it is our responsibility to let Him.

Have you found the lasting peace that can—and should—be yours through Jesus Christ? Or are you still chasing the illusion of "peace and happiness" that the world promises but cannot deliver?

The beautiful words of John 14:27 promise that Jesus offers peace, not as the world gives, but as He alone gives. Your challenge is to welcome Christ's peace into your heart and then, as best you can, to share His peace with your neighbors. But sometimes, that's easier said than done.

> The fruit of our placing all things in God's hands is the presence of His abiding peace in our hearts.
>
> *Hannah Whitall Smith*

If you are a person with lots of obligations and plenty of responsibilities, it is simply a fact of life: You worry. From time to time, you worry about finances, safety, health, home, family, or about countless other concerns, some great and some small. Where is the best place to take your worries? Take them to God . . . and leave them there.

The Scottish preacher George McDonald observed, "It has been well said that no man ever sank under the burden of the day. It is when tomorrow's burden is added to the burden of today that the weight is more than a man can bear. Never load yourselves so, my friends. If you find yourselves so loaded, at least remember this: it is your own doing, not God's. He begs you to leave the future to Him."

Today, as a gift to yourself, to your family, and to your friends, claim the inner peace that is your spiritual birthright: the peace of Jesus Christ. Christ is standing at the door, waiting patiently for you to invite Him to reign over your heart. His eternal peace is offered freely. Claim it today.

A LESSON TO THINK ABOUT

Jesus offers peace that passes human understanding . . . and He wants you to make His peace your peace.

WHAT GOD'S WORD SAYS ABOUT PEACE

The result of righteousness will be peace; the effect of righteousness will be quiet confidence forever.

Isaiah 32:17 Holman CSB

Peace, peace to you, and peace to him who helps you, for your God helps you.

1 Chronicles 12:18 Holman CSB

Grace, mercy, and peace will be with us from God the Father and from Jesus Christ, the Son of the Father, in truth and love.

2 John 1:3 Holman CSB

And let the peace of the Messiah, to which you were also called in one body, control your hearts. Be thankful.

Colossians 3:15 Holman CSB

But now in Christ Jesus, you who were far away have been brought near by the blood of the Messiah. For He is our peace, who made both groups one and tore down the dividing wall of hostility.

Ephesians 2:13-14 Holman CSB

WORDS OF WISDOM ABOUT PEACE

To know God as He really is—in His essential nature and character—is to arrive at a citadel of peace that circumstances may storm, but can never capture.

Catherine Marshall

That peace, which has been described and which believers enjoy, is a participation of the peace which their glorious Lord and Master himself enjoys.

Jonathan Edwards

There may be no trumpet sound or loud applause when we make a right decision, just a calm sense of resolution and peace.

Gloria Gaither

A great many people are trying to make peace, but that has already been done. God has not left it for us to do; all we have to do is to enter into it.

D. L. Moody

Notes to Yourself: _____

_____

_____

_____

_____

_____

_____

_____

_____

_____

_____

_____

_____

As you consider the things you've written in the space above, ask yourself these questions:

Do I believe that God offers me the opportunity to experience a peace that passes human understanding?

Do I conduct myself in ways that will lead to a more peaceful life?

Do I find that my life is more peaceful when I spend more time in prayer and meditation?

YOUR SEARCH FOR MEANING MUST INCLUDE GOD

"I am the bread of life," Jesus told them.
"No one who comes to Me will ever be hungry,
and no one who believes in Me will ever be thirsty again."

John 6:35 Holman CSB

The Message

Jesus said that He was the answer to man's search for meaning and significance.

The sooner we discover what God intends for us to do with our days, the better. But God's purposes aren't always clear to us. Sometimes we wander aimlessly in a spiritual desert of our own making. And sometimes, we struggle stubbornly against God in a futile effort to discover fulfillment and happiness through our own means, not His.

Whenever we resist God's purposes, we are frustrated, and our efforts bear little fruit. But when we genuinely seek His wisdom—and when we follow God's Son wherever He chooses to lead us—the Creator blesses us in unexpected ways.

> Continually restate to yourself what the purpose of your life is.
>
> *Oswald Chambers*

How can we know precisely what God's intentions are? The answer, of course, is that we can't always know exactly what God intends for us to do. Even the most saintly among us will experience periods of uncertainty and doubt. Sometimes, outside circumstances will force us to reevaluate our lives; on other occasions, we may become frustrated, not by the turbulence of life, but by its sameness. In either case, we may find ourselves searching for new direction. If we are wise, we turn to God for that direction.

Are you earnestly seeking to discern God's plans and purposes for your life? If so, remember these important facts: 1. God has wonderful plans in store for you; 2. If you petition God sincerely and prayerfully, you will discern His will; 3. When you discover God's purpose for your life, you will experience abundance, peace, fulfillment, and joy.

And rest assured: when God's purpose becomes your purpose, He will bless you, He will use you, and He will keep you—now and forever.

A LESSON TO THINK ABOUT

When you gain a clear vision of your purpose for life here on earth—and for life everlasting—your steps will be sure.

WHAT GOD'S WORD SAYS ABOUT PURPOSE

Whatever you do, do all to the glory of God.

1 Corinthians 10:31 NKJV

You're sons of Light, daughters of Day. We live under wide open skies and know where we stand. So let's not sleepwalk through life . . . .

1 Thessalonians 5:5-6 MSG

We look at this Son and see the God who cannot be seen. We look at this Son and see God's original purpose in everything created.

Colossians 1:15 MSG

To everything there is a season, a time for every purpose under heaven.

Ecclesiastes 3:1 NKJV

There is one thing I always do. Forgetting the past and straining toward what is ahead, I keep trying to reach the goal and get the prize for which God called me . . . .

Philippians 3:13–14 NCV

WORDS OF WISDOM ABOUT PURPOSE

When God speaks to you through the Bible, prayer, circumstances, the church, or in some other way, he has a purpose in mind for your life.

Henry Blackaby and Claude King

God wants to revolutionize our lives—by showing us how knowing Him can be the most powerful force to help us become all we want to be.

Bill Hybels

Whatever purpose motivates your life, it must be something big enough and grand enough to make the investment worthwhile.

Warren Wiersbe

The worst thing that laziness does is rob a man of spiritual purpose.

Billy Graham

Notes to Yourself: _____

_____

_____

_____

_____

_____

_____

_____

_____

_____

_____

_____

As you consider the things you've written in the space above, ask yourself these questions:

Do I understand the importance of discovering God's unfolding purpose for my life?

Do I consult God on matters great and small?

Do I pray about my plans for the future, and do I remain open to the opportunities and challenges that God places before me?

TAKE TIME TO RECHARGE YOUR BATTERIES

*Come to Me, all you who are weary and burdened,
and I will give you rest. Take My yoke upon you and learn
from Me, because I am gentle and humble in heart,
and you will find rest for your souls.
For My yoke is easy and My burden is light.*

Matthew 11:28-30 Holman CSB

The Message

Jesus offers peace and rest. Jesus brings simplicity. Jesus is the answer to exhaustion and burnout.

Physical exhaustion is God's way of telling us to slow down. God expects us to work hard, of course, but He also intends for us to rest. When we fail to take the rest that we need, we do a disservice to ourselves and to our families.

We live in a world that tempts us to stay up late—very late. But too much late-night TV, combined with too little sleep, is a prescription for exhaustion.

Jesus promises us that when we come to Him, He will give us rest—but we, too, must do our part. We must take the necessary steps to insure that we have sufficient rest and that we take care of our bodies in other ways, too.

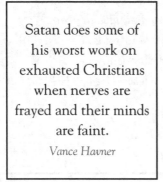

Satan does some of his worst work on exhausted Christians when nerves are frayed and their minds are faint.

Vance Havner

As adults, each of us bears a personal responsibility for the general state of our own physical health. Certainly, various aspects of health are beyond our control: illness sometimes strikes even the healthiest men and women. But for most of us, physical health is a choice: it is the result of hundreds of small decisions that we make every day of our lives. If we make decisions that promote good health, our bodies respond.

But if we fall into bad habits and undisciplined lifestyles, we suffer tragic consequences.

Are your physical or spiritual batteries running low? Is your energy on the wane? Are your emotions frayed? If so, it's time to turn your thoughts and your prayers to God's Son. And when you're finished, it's probably time to turn off the lights and go to bed!

A LESSON TO THINK ABOUT

God wants you to get enough rest. The world wants you to burn the candle at both ends. Trust God.

WHAT GOD'S WORD SAYS ABOUT REST

And the apostles gathered themselves together unto Jesus, and told him all things, both what they had done, and what they had taught. And he said unto them, Come ye yourselves apart into a desert place, and rest a while.

Mark 6:30-31 Holman CSB

He makes me to lie down in green pastures; He leads me beside the still waters. He restores my soul; He leads me in the paths of righteousness for His name's sake.

Psalm 23:2-3 NKJV

I find rest in God; only he gives me hope.

Psalm 62:5 NCV

I said to myself, "Relax and rest. God has showered you with blessings."

Psalm 116:7 MSG

Full of hope, you'll relax, confident again; you'll look around, sit back, and take it easy.

Job 11:18 MSG

WORDS OF WISDOM ABOUT
REST

Jesus gives us the ultimate rest, the confidence we need, to escape the frustration and chaos of the world around us.

Billy Graham

Jesus taught us by example to get out of the rat race and recharge our batteries.

Barbara Johnson

Life is strenuous. See that your clock does not run down.

Mrs. Charles E. Cowman

One reason so much American Christianity is a mile wide and an inch deep is that Christians are simply tired. Sometimes you need to kick back and rest for Jesus' sake.

Dennis Swanberg

Notes to Yourself: _____

_____

_____

_____

_____

_____

_____

_____

_____

_____

_____

_____

_____

As you consider the things you've written in the space above, ask yourself these questions:

Do I understand the importance of getting enough rest each night?

Am I willing to forego other activities in order to go to bed at a sensible hour?

Do I take seriously God's instruction to treat the Sabbath as a day of rest, reflection, and worship?

PRAY MORE

Very early in the morning, while it was still dark,
He got up, went out, and made His way to a deserted place.
And He was praying there.

Mark 1:35 Holman CSB

The Message

Jesus prayed early and often. He engaged in a constant conversation with His Father . . . and we should do likewise.

Does prayer play an important role in your life? Is prayer an integral part of your daily routine, or is it a hit-or-miss activity? Do you "pray without ceasing," or is your prayer life an afterthought? If you genuinely wish to receive that abundance that Christ promises in John 10:10, then you must pray constantly . . . and you must never underestimate the power of prayer.

> When you ask God to do something, don't ask timidly; put your whole heart into it.
>
> *Marie T. Freeman*

As you contemplate the quality of your prayer life, here are a few things to consider: 1. God hears our prayers and answers them (Jeremiah 29:11-12). 2. God promises that the prayers of righteous men and women can accomplish great things (James 5:16). 3. God invites us to be still and to feel His presence (Psalm 46:10).

So pray. Start praying in the early morning and keep praying until you fall off to sleep at night. Pray about matters great and small; and be watchful for the answers that God most assuredly sends your way.

Daily prayer and meditation is a matter of will and habit. When you organize your day to include quiet moments with God, you'll soon discover that no time is more precious than the silent moments you spend with Him.

The quality of your spiritual life will be in direct proportion to the quality of your prayer life. So do yourself a favor: instead of turning things over in your mind, turn them over to God in prayer. Instead of worrying about your next decision, ask God to lead the way. Don't limit your prayers to meals or to bedtime. Pray constantly because God is listening—and He wants to hear from you. And without question, you need to hear from Him.

A LESSON TO THINK ABOUT

Prayer changes things—and it changes you—so pray.

WHAT GOD'S WORD SAYS ABOUT PRAYER

Rejoice evermore. Pray without ceasing. In every thing give thanks: for this is the will of God in Christ Jesus concerning you.

1 Thessalonians 5:16-18 KJV

The effective prayer of a righteous man can accomplish much.

James 5:16 NASB

Whatever you ask for in prayer, believe that you have received it, and it will be yours.

Mark 11:24 NIV

I sought the LORD, and he heard me, and delivered me from all my fears.

Psalm 34:4 KJV

Ask and it shall be given to you; seek and you shall find; knock and it shall be opened to you. For every one who asks receives, and he who seeks finds, and to him who knocks it shall be opened.

Matthew 7:7-8 NASB

WORDS OF WISDOM ABOUT PRAYER

When there is a matter that requires definite prayer, pray until you believe God and until you can thank Him for His answer.

Hannah Whitall Smith

I live in the spirit of prayer; I pray as I walk, when I lie down, and when I rise. And, the answers are always coming.

George Mueller

As we join together in prayer, we draw on God's enabling might in a way that multiplies our own efforts many times over.

Shirley Dobson

The center of power is not to be found in summit meetings or in peace conferences. It is not in Peking or Washington or the United Nations, but rather where a child of God prays in the power of the Spirit for God's will to be done in her life, in her home, and in the world around her.

Ruth Bell Graham

Notes to Yourself: _____

_____

_____

_____

_____

_____

_____

_____

_____

_____

_____

_____

As you consider the things you've written in the space above, ask yourself these questions:

Do I understand that prayer strengthens my relationship with God?

Do I trust that God will care for me, even when it seems that my prayers have gone unanswered?

Do I believe that my prayers have the power to change my circumstances, my perspective, and my future?

SHARE GOD'S GOOD NEWS

Then He said to them,
"Go into all the world and preach the gospel
to the whole creation."

Mark 16:15 Holman CSB

The Message

Jesus clearly instructs us to go out into the world and share His Good News. Each of us can be a spokesperson for Christ—and that's precisely what each of us must do.

A re you a bashful Christian, one who is afraid to speak up for your Savior? Do you allow others to share their testimonies while you stand on the sidelines, reluctant to share yours? After His resurrection, Jesus addressed His disciples:

But the eleven disciples proceeded to Galilee, to the mountain which Jesus had designated. When they saw Him, they worshiped Him; but some were doubtful. And Jesus came up and spoke to them, saying, "All authority has been given to Me in heaven and on earth. 'Go therefore and make disciples of all the nations, baptizing them in the name of the Father and the Son and the Holy Spirit, teaching them to observe all that I commanded you; and lo, I am with you always, even to the end of the age.'" (Matthew 28:16–20 NASB)

> *I will also make You a light of the nations so that My salvation may reach to the end of the earth.*
> Isaiah 49:6 NASB

Christ's great commission applies to Christians of every generation, including our own. As believers, we are called to share the Good News of Jesus Christ with our families, with our neighbors, and with the world. Yet many of us are slow to obey the last commandment of the risen Christ; we simply don't do our best to "make disciples of all the nations." Although our personal testimonies are vitally important, we sometimes hesitate to share our experiences. And that's unfortunate.

Billy Graham observed, "Our faith grows by expression. If we want to keep our faith, we must share it." If you are a follower of Christ, the time to express your belief in Him is now.

You know how Jesus has touched your heart; help Him do the same for others. You must do likewise, and you must do so today. Tomorrow may indeed be too late.

A LESSON TO THINK ABOUT

God's Word clearly instructs you to share His Good News with the world. If you're willing, God will empower you to share your faith.

WHAT GOD'S WORD SAYS ABOUT MISSIONS

Now then we are ambassadors for Christ . . . .

2 Corinthians 5:20 KJV

After this the Lord appointed 70 others, and He sent them ahead of Him in pairs to every town and place where He Himself was about to go. He told them: "The harvest is abundant, but the workers are few. Therefore, pray to the Lord of the harvest to send out workers into His harvest. Now go; I'm sending you out like lambs among wolves."

Luke 10:1-3 Holman CSB

And I say to you, anyone who acknowledges Me before men, the Son of Man will also acknowledge him before the angels of God; but whoever denies Me before men will be denied before the angels of God.

Luke 12:8-9 Holman CSB

This good news of the kingdom will be proclaimed in all the world as a testimony to all nations.

Matthew 24:14 Holman CSB

Words of Wisdom About Missions

The evangelistic harvest is always urgent. The destiny of men and of nations is always being decided. Every generation is strategic. We are not responsible for the past generation, and we cannot bear the full responsibility for the next one, but we do have our generation. God will hold us responsible as to how well we fulfill our responsibilities to this age and take advantage of our opportunities.

Billy Graham

Our commission is quite specific. We are told to be His witness to all nations. For us, as His disciples, to refuse any part of this commission frustrates the love of Jesus Christ, the Son of God.

Catherine Marshall

We are now, a very, very few feeble workers, scattering the grain broadcast according as time and strength permit. God will give the harvest; doubt it not. But the laborers are few.

Lottie Moon

God is not saving the world; it is done. Our business is to get men and women to realize it.

Oswald Chambers

Notes to Yourself: _____

_____

_____

_____

_____

_____

_____

_____

_____

_____

_____

_____

_____

_____

As you consider the things you've written in the space above, ask yourself these questions:

Do I genuinely appreciate the importance of sharing God's message with the world?

Do I believe that God will empower me to share my faith?

Am I willing to look for unplanned opportunities to share the Good News of Jesus Christ?

TRUST
GOD'S WILL

My Father! If it is possible, let this cup pass from Me.
Yet not as I will, but as You will.

Matthew 26:39 Holman CSB

The Message

As He contemplated His death, Jesus accepted God's
will. We, too, must learn to trust the Father completely
and without reservation.

When Jesus confronted the reality of His impending death on the cross, He asked God that this terrible burden might be lifted. But as He faced the possibility of a suffering that was beyond description, Jesus prayed, "Nevertheless not my will, but thine, be done" (Luke 22:42 KJV). As Christians, we, too, must be willing to accept God's will, even when we do not fully understand the reasons for the hardships that we must endure.

As human beings with limited understanding, we can never fully understand the will of God. But as believers in a benevolent God, we must always trust the will of our Heavenly Father. When we trust God, we should trust Him without reservation. We should steel ourselves against the inevitable disappointments of today, secure in the knowledge that our Heavenly Father has a plan for the future that only He can see.

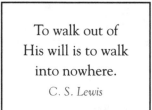

To walk out of His will is to walk into nowhere.

C. S. Lewis

Grief and suffering visit all of us who live long and love deeply. When we lose a loved one, or when we experience any other profound loss, darkness overwhelms us for a while, and it seems as if we cannot summon the strength to face another day—but, with God's help, we can.

When we confront circumstances that trouble us to the very core of our souls, we must trust God. When we are worried, we must turn our concerns over to Him. When we are anxious, we must be still and listen for the quiet assurance of God's promises. And then, by placing our lives in His hands, we learn that He is our shepherd today and throughout eternity. Let us trust the Shepherd.

A LESSON TO THINK ABOUT

Even when you cannot understand God's plans, you must trust them. If you place yourself in the center of God's will, He will provide for your needs and direct your path.

WHAT GOD'S WORD SAYS ABOUT GOD'S WILL

He is the Lord. He will do what He thinks is good.

1 Samuel 3:18 Holman CSB

Teach me your ways, O LORD, that I may live according to your truth! Grant me purity of heart, that I may honor you.

Psalm 86:11 NLT

Commit your activities to the Lord and your plans will be achieved.

Proverbs 16:3 Holman CSB

And this world is fading away, along with everything it craves. But if you do the will of God, you will live forever.

1 John 2:17 NLT

Whoever does the will of God is My brother and sister and mother.

Mark 3:35 Holman CSB

WORDS OF WISDOM ABOUT
GOD'S WILL

Our sense of joy, satisfaction, and fulfillment in life increases, no matter what the circumstances, if we are in the center of God's will.

Billy Graham

The will of God is never exactly what you expect it to be. It may seem to be much worse, but in the end it's going to be a lot better and a lot bigger.

Elisabeth Elliot

Jesus yielded Himself to the Father's will. He was a model of "reverent submission." Jesus lived a life of prayer, faith, and obedience.

Shirley Dobson

Absolute submission is not enough; we should go on to joyful acquiescence to the will of God.

C. H. Spurgeon

Notes to Yourself: _____

_____

_____

_____

_____

_____

_____

_____

_____

_____

_____

_____

As you consider the things you've written in the space above, ask yourself these questions:

Do I believe that God views the world with an eternal perspective that is impossible for me—or anyone else—to grasp?

Do I trust God's will even when I cannot understand it?

Am I willing to accept God's unfolding plan for the world—and for my world?

YOU HAVE A PLACE IN HEAVEN

*In My Father's house are many dwelling places;
if not, I would have told you. I am going away to prepare
a place for you. If I go away and prepare a place for you,
I will come back and receive you to Myself,
so that where I am you may be also.*

John 14:2-3 Holman CSB

The Message

Jesus promises that He has gone to prepare an eternal resting place, and He promises that He will return and carry His children home.

Sometimes life's inevitable troubles and heartbreaks are easier to tolerate when we remind ourselves that heaven is our true home. An old hymn contains the words, "This world is not my home; I'm just passing through." Thank goodness!

For believers, death is not an ending; it is a beginning. For believers, the grave is not a final resting-place; it is a place of transition. Death can never claim those who have accepted Christ as their personal Savior. Christ has promised that He has gone to prepare a glorious home in heaven—a timeless, blessed gift to His children—and Jesus always keeps His promises.

> Heaven itself will reflect the character of our great God. It will be a place of holiness, righteousness, love, justice, mercy, peace, order, and His sovereign rule.
>
> *Bill Bright*

If you've committed your life to Christ, your time here on earth is merely a preparation for a far different life to come: your eternal life with Jesus and a host of fellow believers.

So, while this world can be a place of temporary hardship and temporary suffering, you can be comforted in the knowledge that God offers you a permanent home that is free from all suffering and pain.

Please take God at His word. When you do, you can withstand any problem, knowing that your troubles are temporary, but that heaven is not.

A LESSON TO THINK ABOUT

God has created heaven and given you a way to get there. The rest is up to you.

WHAT GOD'S WORD SAYS ABOUT HEAVEN

Your kingdom is an everlasting kingdom, and Your dominion endures throughout all generations.

Psalm 145:13 NASB

He also raised us up with Him and seated us with Him in the heavens, in Christ Jesus, so that in the coming ages He might display the immeasurable riches of His grace in His kindness to us in Christ Jesus.

Ephesians 2:6-7 Holman CSB

Be glad and rejoice, because your reward is great in heaven.

Matthew 5:12 Holman CSB

Our citizenship is in heaven, from which we also eagerly wait for a Savior, the Lord Jesus Christ.

Philippians 3:20 Holman CSB

As you go, preach this message: "The kingdom of heaven is near."

Matthew 10:7 NIV

Words of Wisdom About Heaven

One of these days, our Father will scoop us up in His strong arms and we will hear Him say those sweet and comforting words, "Come on, child. We're going home."

Gloria Gaither

Considering how I prepare for my children when I know they are coming home, I love to think of the preparations God is making for my homecoming one day. He knows the colors I love, the scenery I enjoy, the things that make me happy, all the personal details.

Anne Graham Lotz

The believing Christian has hope as he stands at the grave of a loved one who is with the Lord, for he knows that the separation is not forever. It is a glorious truth that those who are in Christ never see each other for the last time.

Billy Graham

What joy that the Bible tells us the great comfort that the best is yet to be. Our outlook goes beyond this world.

Corrie ten Boom

Notes to Yourself: _____

_____

_____

_____

_____

_____

_____

_____

_____

_____

_____

_____

As you consider the things you've written in the space above, ask yourself these questions:

Do I believe that Jesus has gone to prepare a place for me in heaven?

Am I secure in my relationship with Jesus, and do I believe that I will have a home with Him throughout eternity?

Do I view death as a transition from mortality to immortality?

SELECTED BIBLE VERSES CONTAINING THE WORDS OF JESUS

ARRANGED BY TOPIC

Abundance

I am come that they might have life, and that they might have it more abundantly.

John 10:10 KJV

These things have I spoken unto you, that my joy might remain in you, and that your joy might be full.

John 15:11 KJV

Whoever has will be given more, and he will have an abundance.

Matthew 13:12 NIV

The master was full of praise. "Well done, my good and faithful servant. You have been faithful in handling this small amount, so now I will give you many more responsibilities. Let's celebrate together!"

Matthew 25:21 NLT

Anger

You have heard that the law of Moses says, 'Do not murder. If you commit murder, you are subject to judgment.' But I say, if you are angry with someone, you are subject to judgment!"

Matthew 5:21 NLT

But I tell you, everyone who is angry with his brother will be subject to judgment.

Matthew 5:22 Holman CSB

You have heard it said, "Love your neighbor and hate your enemy." But I tell you: Love your enemies and pray for those who persecute you, that you may be sons of your Father in heaven.

Matthew 5:43-45 NIV

ASKING GOD

Ask, and it will be given to you; seek, and you will find; knock, and it will be opened to you. For everyone who asks receives, and he who seeks finds, and to him who knocks it will be opened.

Matthew 7:7-8 NKJV

Ye have not chosen me, but I have chosen you, and ordained you, that ye should go and bring forth fruit, and that your fruit should remain; that whatsoever ye shall ask of the Father in my name, he may give it you.

John 15:16 KJV

Behavior

I tell you the truth, whoever believes in me will do the same things that I do. Those who believe will do even greater things than these, because I am going to the Father.

John 14:12 NCV

A good person produces good deeds from a good heart, and an evil person produces evil deeds from an evil heart. Whatever is in your heart determines what you say.

Luke 6:45 NLT

For whosoever shall do the will of God, the same is my brother, and my sister, and mother.

Mark 3:35 KJV

Belief

Jesus said, "Because you have seen Me, you have believed. Blessed are those who believe without seeing."

John 20:29 Holman CSB

Then Jesus told the centurion, "Go. As you have believed, let it be done for you." And his servant was cured that very moment.

Matthew 8:13 Holman CSB

CHRIST'S LOVE

*I am the good shepherd. The good shepherd lays down his life for
the sheep.*

John 10:11 NIV

*Just as the Father has loved Me, I also have loved you. Remain
in My love.*

John 15:9 Holman CSB

And remember, I am with you always, to the end of the age.

Matthew 28:20 Holman CSB

COURAGE

*When they saw Him walking on the sea, they thought it was
a ghost and cried out; for they all saw Him and were terrified.
Immediately He spoke with them and said, "Have courage!
It is I. Don't be afraid."*

Mark 6:49-50 Holman CSB

*But He said to them, "Why are you fearful, O you of little
faith?" Then He arose and rebuked the winds and the sea, and
there was a great calm.*

Matthew 8:26 NKJV

DISCIPLESHIP

"While you have the light, believe in the light, that you may become sons of light." These things Jesus spoke, and departed, and was hidden from them.

John 12:36 NKJV

You did not choose Me, but I chose you. I appointed you that you should go out and produce fruit, and that your fruit should remain, so that whatever you ask the Father in My name, He will give you.

John 15:16 Holman CSB

ETERNAL LIFE

Jesus said to her, "I am the resurrection and the life. The one who believes in Me, even if he dies, will live. Everyone who lives and believes in Me will never die—ever. Do you believe this?"

John 11:25-26 Holman CSB

The one who loves his life will lose it, and the one who hates his life in this world will keep it for eternal life. If anyone serves Me, he must follow Me. Where I am, there My servant also will be. If anyone serves Me, the Father will honor him.

John 12:25-26 Holman CSB

For God so loved the world that He gave His only begotten Son, that whoever believes in Him should not perish but have everlasting life.

John 3:16 NKJV

Most assuredly, I say to you, he who hears My word and believes in Him who sent Me has everlasting life, and shall not come into judgment, but has passed from death into life.

John 5:24 NKJV

FAITH

Anything is possible if a person believes.

Mark 9:23 NLT

Be not faithless, but believing.

John 20:27 KJV

And Jesus answered and said to them, "Truly I say to you, if you have faith and do not doubt, you will not only do what was done to the fig tree, but even if you say to this mountain, 'Be taken up and cast into the sea,' it will happen."

Matthew 21:21 NASB

FORGIVENESS

Be merciful, just as your Father also is merciful.

Luke 6:36 Holman CSB

And forgive us our sins, for we ourselves also forgive everyone in debt to us.

Luke 11:4 Holman CSB

Then Peter came to Him and said, "Lord, how many times could my brother sin against me and I forgive him? As many as seven times?" "I tell you, not as many as seven," Jesus said to him, "but 70 times seven."

Matthew 18:21-22 Holman CSB

Blessed are the merciful, for they will be shown mercy.

Matthew 5:7 NIV

GENEROSITY

Give to everyone who asks from you, and from one who takes away your things, don't ask for them back.

Luke 6:30 Holman CSB

Freely you have received, freely give.

Matthew 10:8 NKJV

GOD

Remember what I told you: I am going away, but I will come back to you again. If you really love me, you will be very happy for me, because now I can go to the Father, who is greater than I am.

John 14:28 NLT

God is Spirit, and those who worship Him must worship in spirit and truth.

John 4:24 Holman CSB

For it is written, "You shall worship the Lord your God, and Him only you shall serve."

Matthew 4:10 NKJV

GOD'S LOVE

The one who has My commandments and keeps them is the one who loves Me. And the one who loves Me will be loved by My Father. I also will love him and will reveal Myself to him.

John 14:21 Holman CSB

Greater love has no one than this, than to lay down one's life for his friends.

John 15:13 NKJV

GOD'S SUPPORT

Take My yoke upon you and learn from Me, because I am gentle and humble in heart, and you will find rest for your souls. For My yoke is easy and My burden is light.

Matthew 11:29-30 Holman CSB

Jesus looked at them and said, "With man this is impossible, but with God all things are possible."

Matthew 19:26 NIV

GOD'S WILL

"Father, if it is Your will, take this cup away from Me; nevertheless not My will, but Yours, be done."

Luke 22:42 NKJV

Jesus answered them, and said, "My doctrine is not mine, but his that sent me."

John 7:16 KJV

Jesus replied, "Who is my mother? Who are my brothers?" Then he looked at those around him and said, "These are my mother and brothers. Anyone who does God's will is my brother and sister and mother."

Mark 3:33-35 NLT

God's Word

Heaven and earth will pass away, but My words will never pass away.

Matthew 24:35 Holman CSB

But He answered, "It is written: Man must not live on bread alone, but on every word that comes from the mouth of God."

Matthew 4:4 Holman CSB

The one who is from God listens to God's words. This is why you don't listen, because you are not from God.

John 8:47 Holman CSB

Great Commandment

Jesus replied, "'Love the Lord your God with all your heart and with all your soul and with all your mind.' This is the first and greatest commandment. And the second is like it: 'Love your neighbor as yourself.' All the Law and the Prophets hang on these two commandments."

Matthew 22:37-40 NIV

Great Commission

Go, therefore, and make disciples of all nations, baptizing them in the name of the Father and of the Son and of the Holy Spirit, teaching them to observe everything I have commanded you. And remember, I am with you always, to the end of the age.

Matthew 28:19-20 Holman CSB

Greed

And He said to them, "Take heed and beware of covetousness, for one's life does not consist in the abundance of the things he possesses."

Luke 12:15 NKJV

No one can be a slave of two masters, since either he will hate one and love the other, or be devoted to one and despise the other. You cannot be slaves of God and of money.

Matthew 6:24 Holman CSB

Grief

Blessed are you who are hungry now, because you will be filled. Blessed are you who weep now, because you will laugh.

Luke 6:21 Holman CSB

So you also have sorrow now. But I will see you again. Your hearts will rejoice, and no one will rob you of your joy.

John 16:22 Holman CSB

These things I have spoken unto you, that in me ye might have peace. In the world ye shall have tribulation: but be of good cheer; I have overcome the world.

John 16:33 KJV

HEAVEN

In My Father's house are many dwelling places; if not, I would have told you. I am going away to prepare a place for you. If I go away and prepare a place for you, I will come back and receive you to Myself, so that where I am you may be also.

John 14:2-3 Holman CSB

As you go, preach this message: "The kingdom of heaven is near."

Matthew 10:7 NIV

Again, the kingdom of heaven is like a merchant in search of fine pearls. When he found one priceless pearl, he went and sold everything he had, and bought it.

Matthew 13:45-46 Holman CSB